BASIC SCHOOLING
MADE SIMPLE

BASIC SCHOOLING MADE SIMPLE

MARTIN DIGGLE *AND* MAGGIE RAYNOR

J. A. ALLEN
LONDON

First published in Great Britain 2002

ISBN 0 85131 043 0

J.A. Allen
Clerkenwell House
Clerkenwell Green
London EC1R 0HT

J.A. Allen is an imprint of Robert Hale Ltd

British Library Cataloguing in Publication Data
A catalogue record for this book is available from the British Library

Design by Nancy Lawrence
Colour separation by Tenon & Polert Colour Scanning Ltd
Printed in Singapore by Kyodo Printing

CONTENTS

PREFACE

Seat is obviously an essential element in mastery of the horse,
but the rider's head is surely as important as his seat.
Ulrik Schramm

This book has been written primarily for the novice owner (or potential owner), who wishes to train their much-loved –– but not necessarily perfect –– horse to best effect.

When training any horse, it is important to take account of that horse's individual characteristics, both mental and physical. This is especially true of horses whose conformation falls short of the ideal. However willing their nature, there may be some things that they will find inevitably difficult to do in 'textbook' fashion. Making unthinking demands of such horses will not only set up avoidable resistances and damage the horse/rider relationship – it is also distinctly unfair. One main aim of this book is, therefore, to help the reader evaluate what their particular horse can reasonably be expected to do, and to develop his training positively along the lines of what is practical. In a similar vein, the book seeks to help readers who have acquired less-than-perfect horses, upon whom unreasonable demands have previously been made, to deal with any inherited flaws and to re-establish training along the right lines.

The other partner in the training process is, of course, the rider. This book makes the point that *all* riding is training and that the horse cannot be expected to do what is required of him if he is given a series of confused or contradictory signals. It therefore gives guidance on correct basic posture and on applying the aids both thoughtfully and accurately.

In dealing with progressive training and explaining various exercises, the text makes reference to the requirements of basic level dressage tests. While the emphasis is on dressage as training, rather than as a competitive discipline, it is hoped that the book will help readers who do wish to compete, whether on a regular or more occasional basis. With this in mind, the final chapter deals with the practicalities of preparing for, and riding, a test.

Our main intention in writing this book is, however, to help readers to discover the best way to train *their* particular horse, so that they can establish a happy partnership, that progresses successfully in whatever they choose to do.

Note for readers outside Britain: This book makes reference to British Dressage, which is the national governing body for the sport in Britain, and runs affiliated competitions. It also refers to British Eventing, which organises dressage as a phase of horse trials, and to the Riding and Pony Club movements, which run dressage competitions primarily for their own members and generally at a local level. The rules of these other bodies follow those of British Dressage closely, but are not necessarily identical in all points of detail. This general structure of a national governing body and other specialised or 'local' bodies is reflected in many other countries, and readers should substitute the names of the British organisations with their own equivalents. For example, in America the governing body is USA Equestrian, and the Pony Club equivalent is United States Pony Clubs.

Since the national bodies all have close links with the international governing body (the FEI), the principles applied to competition dressage are very similar in most countries. This is true, not only of the major principles of training, but of the principle of providing a progressive range of tests, starting at a basic level and working towards the levels used in international competitions. However, although this principle is universal, the actual tests and the names ascribed to them vary from country to country. In Britain, the two basic levels are known respectively as Preliminary and Novice. These, very approximately, contain the same sort of movements as are found in the various American Training Level tests. Generally speaking, the basic level tests of other countries will contain similar movements. However, in the context of this book, the important point is not to define which movements appear in which tests, but to understand the training value of each movement and the principles of riding it correctly.

INTRODUCTION

This book is intended to help and encourage novice riders who are engaged in the everyday training of their horses, whatever make, shape, type or breed their horses may be. While the book makes reference to preparing for dressage tests up to British Dressage Novice Level, it should be stressed that the movements and exercises discussed are, first and foremost, training exercises. In other words, they are included in dressage tests to *provide evidence of correct training* – they are not simply things to be learnt in order to ride a particular test. Therefore, even if you have no interest at all in competitive dressage, you will still find that using and practising these exercises provides a basis for your training.

It might be useful at this point to clear up a misconception about dressage. Although increasingly popular as a competitive sport, for many people it still has an air of mystery. Indeed, some people think of it as somehow distinct from 'normal' riding. This is by no means the case. While it is true that top-level dressage requires exceptionally talented horses and riders, and years of training, it is no different in this respect from any other sports and art forms. While we may marvel at their level of mastery, the Wimbledon champion is still playing tennis, the concert pianist is still playing the piano, and the Olympic dressage champion is still riding a horse.

Although this may seem to be stating the obvious – or even an unhelpful over-simplification – it is actually the key to an important truth. In order to succeed in any sport or art, participants have to adhere to certain principles, certain concepts and practices, that will permit success – and these principles are the same for everyone. The Wimbledon champion who gets out of position or miss-times a shot will hit the ball out, just like the player in the park; the concert pianist who hits a wrong note will produce a discord, just like the amateur thumping out a tune in the pub. The point is that top practitioners do not work to a different set of principles from ordinary mortals – they work to the same principles, but with greater refinement and skill.

So, how does this help the ordinary rider? A great deal, is the answer. In the first place, equitation has been studied intensively for hundreds of years and, during that time, many observant, innovative, analytical and talented people have succeeded in establishing the key principles beyond any reasonable doubt. In other words, the blueprint exists! This is not to say, of course, that training horses has been made easy. It hasn't. It still requires natural talent, acquired skills and lots of patience, practice and experience. Those who reach the upper levels of riding and training do so by progressing gradually down a long road. The good news is first, that the road is well trodden (the signposts, or principles, are in place) and second, that *any* real progress down that road is bound to benefit all horses and riders.

The reason for this is that the whole purpose of dressage is to improve the horse's athleticism, balance and responsiveness to the rider, and these factors are bound to enhance the horse's performance, regardless of whether he is performing a canter pirouette, jumping a corner in a hunter trial, taking part in a gymkhana game or simply walking down a steep, stony path. So we can see that, far from being different from 'normal' riding, dressage is inextricably linked to all branches of equestrian sport.

Indeed the French word *dressage* does not translate into English as 'doing fancy riding tricks in a funny hat', but rather as 'training' (*dresseur* = trainer). In equestrian terms, we can think of training along two lines; physical and mental. In the physical sense, we can think of it as being similar to the physical training of a human athlete – that is to say, influencing the body's ability to perform athletic feats. In the mental sense, we can think of it as influencing how the horse learns to respond to the rider's wishes. It is fundamentally important to realise that whenever we ride we are, to some extent, influencing the horse both physically and mentally, so it follows that, *whenever we ride, we are inevitably training the horse.*

This training may be a conscious act (for example, we may decide to teach a horse to jump ditches), or it may be subconscious (by remaining quiet and calm on a nervous, gassy horse in a difficult situation, we may prevent him from 'boiling over', and help to modify his reaction to a similar situation in the future). Also, our training may be positive (by patience, reassurance and persistence, we persuade a young horse to pass a new, alarming object) or negative (by allowing him to snatch the reins and grab mouthfuls from the hedgerow, we teach a horse bad manners and evasion). The point is, it will be one or the other. *Whatever we tell or allow the horse to do – or provoke him into doing – we will somehow affect his training, for better or worse.* Since this is the case, it makes sense to try to ensure that everything we have to do with the horse has a positive effect on him – in other words, that we train him correctly.

Correct training may be manifest is various ways, but its positive effects apply across the range of equestrian activities. This principle was well understood by the old masters, who recommended that all horses be given a sound (quite advanced) general education before progressing to their intended specialised field. In this modern era, where the tendency is to specialise too much, too soon, it is easy to view horses as 'showjumpers', 'hunters', 'hacks' or 'dressage horses', but this view is generally detrimental to both horse and rider. It tends to impose artificial limits on the horse's overall education, and the expectations it fosters may lead to hurried training and attempted shortcuts, neither of which are ever successful in the long term. (Alternatively, it may lead to a complete lack of training. The rider who 'only wants to hack' may dismiss all but the most rudimentary training as unnecessary, but is in for a rude shock when their crooked, unbalanced horse slips and stumbles down a steep hill, or when their unschooled horse, who ignores both leg and hand, is surrounded by flapping tarpaulins and lorries with hissing airbrakes.)

The first reason for training a horse is, then, necessity. If we are to ride at all, then the horse must have at least a basic education if we are to do anything with reasonable proficiency and safety.

The second reason for training, too often overlooked, is for enjoyment – the pleasure of the process. Nowadays, very few people (and, by definition, no amateurs) *have* to ride horses. We do so from choice, presumably because we enjoy riding. Since, as we have seen, all riding entails training, and training is a necessity, the training process and our enjoyment are (or should be) closely linked. Regardless of our ultimate ambitions in riding, we should enjoy witnessing the horse's development, sensing our heightened two-way communication with him and establishing a partnership – and the horse should enjoy it, too.

It is a heightened concentration upon the training process, in particular the development of the horse's flatwork, that we nowadays term 'dressage', and the tendency is to think of it as a competitive discipline. However, dressage is not specifically competitive; indeed, the competition form is a fairly recent addition to equestrian sport, much of its development having taken place during the twentieth century. Before this, those riders who celebrated the aesthetic and artistic elements of equitation did so largely in non-competitive displays. In recent years, there has been a resurgence of interest in dressage (i.e. schooling) purely for its own sake, and many riders (some of whom are highly talented) gain great satisfaction from this without having any inclination to compete.

On the other hand, a very large numbers of riders do feel the urge to compete, for a variety of reasons. There is the challenge of performing the prescribed movements under test conditions; feedback from different judges, which can provide pointers for training; the chance to compare performances from test to test and to progress through the levels. (Simply having a competitive nature is a reason that requires caution, since dressage is not a sport in which one can influence the performance of others. The trick is to compete against your own past performances, not against other horses and riders.)

But whatever your final goals may be, and regardless of whether you are training your horse for competitive or non-competitive purposes, we hope that the ideas in this book will help you establish a real partnership with your horse and develop his individual potential. That, ultimately, is what training should be about.

· 1 ·

BASIC PRINCIPLES

As mentioned in the introduction, dressage is really a system of progressive training designed to improve the ridden horse's all-round capabilities. The basic principles of dressage can be thought of as the skeleton around which the training system is built up. In a young creature, the basic skeleton is developed at a very early stage. In time, the bones grow and strengthen – certain related ones may even fuse – but the skeleton does not fundamentally change; the thigh bone of the baby remains the thigh bone of the adult.

The basic principles of dressage are similar to this; although they will grow and become fleshed out they continue to apply throughout the whole training programme. As training brings improvement in the horse, this allows the rider to apply the principles to greater effect, but the principles themselves remain the same. One consequence of this is that, because they *are* principles, if a rider starts to ignore one, even at an advanced stage, this will impair training and block progress. Furthermore, a rider who 'skates over' one of the principles at an early stage may appear to get away with it for a while but, sooner or later, a problem will surface, and the rider will have to retrace steps and put right the omission before there can be any hope of successful continuation.

What, then, are the basic principles of dressage? Well, as with most things, there are slightly different ways of describing what are essentially the same ideas. The most succinct description of the qualities essential to training was supplied by the nineteenth-century French master, Alexis-François L'Hotte, in his maxim 'calm, forward and straight'. However, if we are to work toward these criteria, a little elaboration may be in order. Since this book focuses on the basic level dressage tests, and these are tests of training, it may be appropriate to look to these for guidance.

At the bottom of each test sheet, there are several collective marks. These are awarded according to the judge's assessment of certain factors throughout the whole test. The reason why these factors are assessed in this way is that they represent the basis of correct training. Their presence or absence will indicate the quality of a horse's training, and will inevitably influence the way in which individual movements are performed. The factors concerned are defined as follows:

Paces (freedom and regularity)

Impulsion (desire to move forward, elasticity of the steps, suppleness of the back and engagement of the hindquarters)

Submission (attention and confidence; harmony, lightness and ease of movement; acceptance of the bridle and lightness of the forehand)

Rider's position and seat: correctness and effect of the aids.

One of the collective marks always relates to the rider, and we will discuss the rider's role in the next chapter. For the time being, however, let us see what we can learn from the other definitions.

PACES (GAITS)[1]

In the first place, 'freedom' of gaits cannot occur if there is restriction, so we can conclude that correct training involves allowing the horse to move freely; perhaps developing his ability to do so, but obviously not restricting him.

The term 'regularity' seems to back this up. To move well in the different gaits, the horse must move in a regular rhythm: 1.2.3.4. in walk; 1.2,1.2. in trot and 1.2.3, 1.2.3 in canter. It is not hard to see that, if we restrict his movement or, indeed, bustle him along too fast, we may well interfere with freedom and regularity of movement.

Since freedom and regularity are basic requirements, we may also conclude that, if we take on a horse whose movement is somehow impaired, we will have to try to remedy this by appropriate horsemastership, exercise and schooling before we can progress very far.

IMPULSION

Impulsion is defined first as the horse's desire to move forward which, from the rider's viewpoint, is to use his energy in the most positive fashion. All movement requires energy, and the horse must be moving actively forward (or be prepared to do so) in order to perform any ridden movement well. Therefore, the horse's desire to move forward must be considered of fundamental importance.

If impulsion is so important, we should give some thought to its source. To some extent, the horse's desire to move forward is instinctive; he is essentially a creature who roams in search of food and runs away from danger. This instinctive impulsion is inherited in physique, temperament and nervous energy, and so it varies from horse to horse.

The instinctive impulsion that triggers the horse's desire to move forward will be fuelled and powered by physical energy. This, in the first instance, is the energy that the horse's body obtains from food, augmented by gymnastic training that makes the horse stronger and fitter, and his movement more efficient. So, while instinctive impulsion makes the horse *want to move* forward, this second form of 'mechanical' impulsion provides the power for him to do so.

There is another sort of impulsion, which we might call 'imparted'. This produces forward movement only when the rider, to some extent, demands it. In other words, although the horse has a reasonable amount of energy available, he does not offer it freely, but has to be told to use it. Although imparted impulsion can have the required effect of producing active forward movement, it is not really so valuable as the other forms. There are two reasons for this. First, the desire

- *The horse must learn to move in balance whilst carrying the rider, and this process will require the rider to exercise sensitive and subtle support and control. However, when restriction and constraint replace subtle controls, there will always be negative effects upon the horse's balance, rhythm and regularity of movement.*

In picture (a), the rider is restraining forward movement: he is leaning back; his body is behind the vertical and his leg has swung too far forward to give any positive aids. He is also hanging on to the horse's mouth. In consequence, the horse is way above the bit, his back has hollowed and correct, active movement of his hind limbs is impossible. If he does succeed in moving forward, it will be in a manner beyond the rider's control.

In picture (b), the rider is tilted forward and has little use of her seat. Her raised hands and rein contact are causing the horse to come behind the bit. The horse will tend to mince forward in short, inactive strides and, in this position, the rider will be able to do little about it.

In picture (c), the rider is in a correct, upright posture, sitting still, in balance with the horse. His leg is in the correct position to give supporting, or actively driving, aids as necessary, and his quiet hands and light rein contact are inviting the horse to move freely forward. In consequence, the horse is displaying active, balanced movement.

[1] Those responsible for administering competitive dressage in Britain generally refer to walk, trot and canter as 'paces' and, since this is the term used on test sheets, etc., the reader will probably be familiar with this usage. However, in some contexts this may give rise to confusion, since 'pace' also means 'step' or 'speed'. To muddy the waters further, there is also a lateral gait (sequence of footfall) which is actually called 'the pace', or 'pacing'. The term 'gait' describes a particular sequence of footfall far more specifically than 'pace', and it is this former term that is used throughout this book.

(a)

(b)

(c)

(a)

(b)

(c)

to move forward should, ideally, be for its own sake (a sign of willingness). Second, imparting impulsion usually involves some expenditure of the rider's own energies (both mental and physical), which could otherwise be employed in different ways (*using* the horse's energy, rather than demanding it).

Obviously, a rider can only impart impulsion successfully to a horse who actually has some energy to expend so, if we find ourselves working away too hard, we need to ask first, whether the horse actually has the energy for the task in hand and second, if he does, why his desire to go forward is so suppressed. (We will look further at these issues in due course.)

Before leaving this issue of imparted impulsion, we should emphasise the important distinction between a horse *having to be told* to use his energy and a horse *waiting to be told* to use his energy. Obviously, there is a practical sense in which we always want the horse to *wait to be told* to use his energy. We do not, for example, want him to cock his jaw at a busy road junction and run into the path of a juggernaut. Also, there may be times when it is inappropriate for a horse to use all of his available energy too freely. For example, a keen young horse may be willing to offer more energy than his balance,

- *Since all movement requires energy, the horse must be mentally and physically active in order to perform any movement well.*
(a) Active working trot: the horse's demeanour indicates that he is happy to be working; the rider is able to sit still and quiet and just allow the forward movement.
(b) Inactive – the horse is taking short steps and is not reaching forward into the rein contact. The rider, in a slightly slouched position and with her leg a little forward, is doing nothing to encourage further activity. The horse looks to be wondering whether there is anyone on top.
(c) An example of what happens when a stiff, hollow back interferes with the flow of energy. A horse in this outline may scamper along but, because he is unable to engage his hind limbs properly underneath his body, he will not be able to carry and propel himself to best effect.

at that stage of training, may sustain. In such cases, prudence is called for. However, the horse who has a *desire* to move forward can still wait for instructions and do so in the manner decreed by the rider. This is true impulsion coupled with obedience, a very different proposition from the reluctant, inactive horse who always has to be *told* to go about his business.

Looking at the other descriptions associated with impulsion, the first we see is elasticity of the steps. Technically, elasticity is the property which allows a muscle to lengthen, which is actually a passive process, brought about by the contraction of that muscle's 'pair' (skeletal muscles operate in pairs). If we view elasticity of the steps in more general terms as a springy property of the whole horse, we will see that it must be closely related to suppleness (which allows maximum muscular contraction and expansion) and to the physical development of the muscles, which makes them stronger, more efficient 'springs'. Thus we will see that elastic movement is evidence that mechanical impulsion is being developed along the right lines. (If we just gave the horse a lot of energy by overfeeding him, and ignored his gymnastic development, he would simply rush around showing stilted, uncoordinated movement, inability to bend, etc., which is not what we are trying to achieve.)

It is important to emphasise the connection between elastic steps and the springiness of the whole horse, and this brings us to consider suppleness of the back. The horse, obviously, is a single entity, and we want him to move in a coordinated way, in a form that is often termed 'united' or 'connected'. If he is to do this, his elasticity cannot be isolated in his limbs – it must extend throughout the whole horse, especially through his back. (Imagine, for a moment, that the horse's fore and hind limbs were giant bedsprings, but his back was a rigid steel joist. How comfortable would that be to sit on? Also, suppose that the steel joist was capable of sensation – how comfortable would the horse feel, with the perpetually jolted rider bouncing up and down on his back?) However, there is more at stake here than just comfort; there is the whole question of propulsion, and this brings us to the engagement of the hindquarters.

The horse is a 'rear-engined' creature, that is, he is designed to propel himself along chiefly by using his hindquarters. (As training advances and the hindquarters are strengthened, they also develop their 'carrying' role, which leads to collection.) If the horse is to move forward actively and efficiently, he will need to make good use of his back end, 'engaging his hindquarters' and bringing his hind legs well forward underneath himself.

In the horse's anatomy, there are major links of ligament, skeleton and musculature between his back and his hindquarters and these links create interactions. If a horse stiffens and hollows his back (or if it is naturally stiff and hollow), this will block the action of his hind legs. Rather than engage underneath his body, they will more or less scamper along behind him: less energy will be produced and the horse will be compelled to move in a way that is both inefficient and relatively uncomfortable for himself and his rider. He will carry a greater proportion of weight on his forehand and may try to supplement his lack of 'engine power' by dragging himself along with his forelimbs, which are not designed for this function. If, on the other hand, the horse has a supple back, he will be able to engage his hindquarters properly and, as his hind legs step well forward underneath his body, this will increase the tendency of his back to lift and round. Far more energy will be available, the whole horse will move with springy elasticity, and he will carry the rider with greater ease and efficiency. Looking back to the subject of gaits, we can see that it is this second form of progression that is more likely to promote freedom and regularity of movement and, as we shall see in a moment, it is also the form more likely to assist with submission.

SUBMISSION

We can see from the terms used to define submission that this must be a matter of willing acceptance on the horse's part. Qualities such as confidence, harmony, lightness and ease are not consistent with harsh or forceful riding. Indeed, such measures seem more likely to destroy than to produce the qualities required. Common sense suggests that willing acceptance is most likely to come about if the horse understands what is

required of him, is physically capable of doing what he is asked, and finds doing it generally a pleasant – or at least not an unpleasant – experience. Regarding acceptance of the bridle and lightness of the forehand, the latter can only come about if, as we have seen, the horse is engaging his hindquarters. Once this is achieved, he is more likely to show acceptance of the bridle; certainly, he will be less inclined to lean on the rider's hands and the rider, in consequence, will be less inclined to try to counter such leaning by entering into a tug of war.

Overall, then, it is logical to expect submission to improve as the horse learns more thoroughly what is expected of him, and is made fitter and more supple. The conclusion to be drawn is that (although we always need a basic level of obedience from the horse), we do not have to make him submissive in a negative sense *in order* to train him; instead, our training should *enable* him to become more submissive in a positive sense.

Below the collective marks at the bottom of a test sheet, there is a heading 'Purpose of Test', which has sub-headings in respect of the rider and the horse. These list criteria that are applied 'to demonstrate that horse and rider are beginning their training on correct lines'. If we look at these criteria, we will see that they are closely linked to the qualities just discussed, for which the collective marks are awarded. At Novice Level, six of the criteria by which the horse's training is judged are as follows. (The collective mark(s) to which they chiefly relate are added in brackets.)

• *Submission, and lack of submission.*
(a) The horse is moving calmly and willingly forward, with ears pricked.
(b) The horse is restricted by the strong rein contact. His hocks are trailing, he is taking short steps in front and his neck is restricted. A horse will never show the signs of true submission if he is uncomfortable and his movement is being cramped.
(c) Above the bit, crooked and resistant. The posture of a horse who is either frightened, or defying the rider. It is fundamentally important to be sure which is the case when attempting correction.

(a)

(b)

(c)

Has true, regular and unhurried paces (**paces/gaits**).

Is calm, relaxed and obedient to the aids of the rider (**submission**).

Maintains balance and rhythm and a natural rounded outline, without restriction (**paces/gaits, impulsion, submission**).

Moves freely forward without collection but showing a slightly greater degree of engagement than that required at Preliminary Level (**impulsion, submission**).

Accepts the bit willingly and without tension or resistance (**submission**).

Executes transitions smoothly and remains still when halted (**paces/gaits, impulsion, submission**).

In addition to these, there is a seventh criterion, which is that the horse *'remains straight when moving on straight lines and bends accordingly when moving on curved lines'* (i.e. his hind feet follow the tracks made by his forefeet) and this brings us to consider a further principle of training, the issue of straightness.

STRAIGHTNESS

If we refer back, for a moment, to L'Hotte's maxim, 'calm, forward and straight', we will see that the calm, forward aspects are clearly reflected in the qualities already discussed under paces, impulsion and submission. The reason why the key issue of straightness is not addressed specifically in the collective marks is almost certainly because it is inextricably linked to all the individual movements of the test. (For example, movement can only be *truly* regular if the horse is straight – equal on both sides – and straightness, or lack of it, will also impact on factors such as engagement and submission.) While this could also be claimed of the qualities listed in the collective marks, it is perhaps fair to say that they can often be judged more readily in overview. For example, a horse might show a good level of obedience (submission) throughout a test, except for one brief moment of resistance, or he might show a consistently acceptable level of impulsion, except for one or two brief moments in which it is lost. However, since the whole test consists of straight lines, turns and circles, it is quite likely that deficiencies in straightness may show up almost continuously, in varying degrees, throughout the test, with variable impact on the individual movements.

Why is straightness so important? Because it allows the horse to be ambidextrous – to move with equal facility to both left and right, and because it is essential for advanced training. Straightness is, in fact, a prime example of a principle that cannot be ignored. A rider who seeks to advance the horse's training without working progressively on straightness will discover that without it, true collection is impossible and advanced movements such as flying changes and half-pass zigzags cannot be performed correctly and evenly.

There is one aspect of straightness which sets it apart from the other qualities that we seek in training. That is, it is not a natural quality. Many horses have good natural movement; many show instinctive impulsion; many are naturally good-natured and cooperative – but it is virtually impossible to find one who is born truly straight. The reasons for this, and what we have to do about it, will be discussed more fully in Chapter 6.

PHILOSOPHICAL PRINCIPLES

Having looked at some of the technical principles behind training, it may be useful to consider briefly three principles of training philosophy. These appear time after time in the writings of the great masters. They are stated with the utmost clarity, by writers of different generations and nationalities, and we ignore them at our peril. The philosophical principles are:

Layered progression. Training horses is a process built up layer upon layer. You can't build the walls until you have laid the foundations; you can't put the roof on until you have built the walls. If you try to do so, your house will fall down. Not *might* fall down – *will* fall down.

Patience. The greatest trainer in the world can't teach a horse faster than that horse can learn. The greatest trainer in the world wouldn't want to try. Good trainers understand the need to build a horse up gradually, both mentally and physically – they don't want to ask a horse questions that he will struggle to answer, because they know that this will lead to confusion, panic, resentment and resistance – which are not classical signs of submission. So, there are no short cuts – except those that lead to a spoilt horse.

Adherence to the technical principles. This, in effect, encapsulates the two previous principles. The layered progression must be along correct technical lines: you must use the right sort of concrete for your foundations, and the right bricks for your walls. Patience must be tempered with the knowledge that what you are trying to teach the horse is, in fact, correct. The checks involve reference to the technical principles. In our training, we do not always march resolutely down the road to our goal. Sometimes we take faltering, hesitant steps, sometimes we even stop. However, we can always check our work. Is it tending to make the horse calmer, more forward, straighter? If so, then we must be pretty much on the right road. If, however, we find that what we are doing has a markedly different effect – the horse becomes persistently more agitated, resistant, crooked – then this is a clear indication that we need to retrace our steps and get back on course.

· 2 ·

THE RIDER'S TECHNIQUE

We have already established that any rider is, willy-nilly, a trainer, and that the rider's aim must be to train the horse in a positive way. As we have already suggested, and shall discuss further in due course, training is not *only* a matter of riding technique. Nevertheless, it is plain to see that the better we understand *why* we give the aids, and the better we apply them, the better placed we will be to make accurate judgements about the horse's responses. In other words, the more technically proficient a rider is, the more able he or she will be to assess what training is needed, to ride training exercises properly and to evaluate the horse's responses and progress.

THE LOGIC BEHIND THE AIDS

The term 'aids' is commonly used to describe both the parts of the body a rider uses to communicate with the horse and the actual signals sent down these lines of communication. In order to be clear in our minds what we are trying to achieve by applying the aids, it is worth taking a brief look backwards in time to the problems facing the people who first began to ride horses.

A rider is sitting on a horse and wishes to control that horse – how can this be achieved? The obvious answer is that the rider can try to find ways of communicating with the horse by using those parts of their own body that are in contact with the horse – their seat and legs. It is also apparent that it would be helpful to have some communication with the horse's front end – especially his head, which leads his movement. The obvious means of such communication would be via the rider's hands –

especially since the hands are a human's most natural and instinctive form of contact. One possibility might be to try to control the horse by holding on to his ears but (a) this might not work very well and (b) they are a long way forward – trying to reach them would put the rider in a precarious position and would certainly compromise any use of seat and legs. Perhaps it would be better to consider other options, such as the horse's mouth or nose, both of which seem fairly sensitive. Of course, they are even harder to reach than the ears, but perhaps it would be possible to achieve some mechanical link with them – maybe a rope, or leather straps – which would enable the rider to remain secure and upright on the horse's back.

Another possible means of communication to consider is the voice. This is the main method that human beings use to communicate with one another and it also works, to some extent, with other domesticated animals. It might, therefore, be worth a try with the horse.

Once these possibilities have been recognised, the next step is to decide how they can be employed to obtain consistent results. Logically, there are two main points to consider. First, what can the rider actually *do* with these lines of contact and second, how can the choice of actions be related to the horse's conformation, senses and instincts, so that what the rider does will convey signals which the horse can recognise, understand and obey.

These are the questions which occurred thousands of years ago and, down through the ages, the most thoughtful and skilful riders discovered that they could, indeed, communicate with the horse through the means of contact outlined. In fact, as they refined their methods, they discovered that they could exercise a remarkable degree of control – correctly trained, a horse could become amazingly sensitive and responsive to their signals.

There is, however, another side to this. If a horse can be highly sensitive to *correctly applied* aids, it follows that he will also be sensitive to – and confused by – *incorrectly applied* aids. Let us, therefore, give some thought to the basic aids as we now know them and see how they can be applied in either a positive or a negative way.

THE SEAT

THE SEAT AND POSTURE

Before looking at the seat as an aid in itself, we should take note of its other crucial function. The seat – the way in which a rider sits in the saddle – is the foundation of the rider's whole posture; indeed, good posture is often referred to as a 'good seat'. It is necessary to understand that this good seat is not primarily a matter of being stylish or looking good – it is essential for much more important reasons. These are:

1. It provides maximum security for the rider. This, desirable for its own sake, also means that the rider is less likely to use the legs and hands incorrectly for gripping or hanging on.
2. It places the rider in a position which maximises balance and harmony with the horse (which, in turn, makes it easier for the horse to keep his own balance, and therefore easier for him to respond correctly to the rider's aids).
3. It places the rider in the position from which all the aids can be applied most effectively (hence the collective mark on the test sheet for 'rider's position and seat, correctness and effect of the aids'). This is because a correct seat (consisting of upper thighs, buttocks, pelvis and lower back) provides a firm base of support for the upper body and also acts as a shock absorber, insulating the upper body from the effects of the horse's movement so that it, and the hands, can remain quiet and still. As mentioned above, the legs are freed from any tendency to grip and enabled to apply the full range of aids.

HOW THE SEAT AIDS WORK

The ways in which the seat itself works as an aid relate to the rider's weight and the horse's balance. Although a horse is a lot bigger than a person, a rider is still a considerable weight on a horse's back. Like any other creature, a horse will instinctively wish to keep his balance and, when he has a weight on his back, he has to take this, as well as his own mass and movement, into account in order to do so. Therefore, if the weight on his back shifts in any direction, the horse's instinct is to adjust his own movement in response.

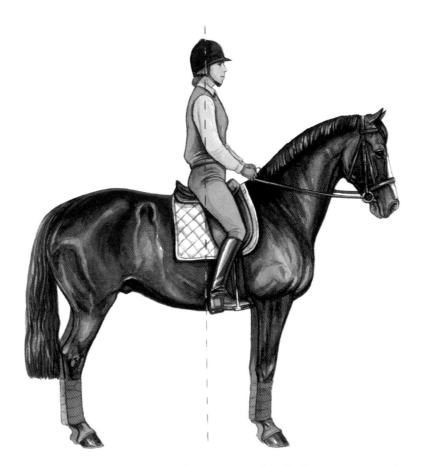

● *Correct posture is not merely a matter of style. It maximises rider security, harmonises the balance of horse and rider and places the rider in the best position from which to apply the aids effectively.*

When correctly seated, a rider's weight is almost vertically over the horse's centre of motion (the midpoint along the horse's spine between his forelegs and hind legs). This positioning above such a key point means that the way in which the rider's weight is brought to bear has a considerable influence in encouraging or restraining the horse's forward movement, or in influencing his sideways movement.

When considering the effectiveness of the seat as an aid we should remember that an apparently small signal from the seat itself is reinforced by the weight of the rider above it. In addition, we should remember that the horse has the simple capacity to feel through his back, via his nervous system. Not only will he feel major changes in weight or pressure (such as an unbalanced rider thumping down on his back), he will also feel minor changes, such as a rider flexing or relaxing muscles in the seat. He can, by association, learn to interpret such changes in the same way as he can learn to interpret subtle changes in leg or rein aids. Therefore, if the seat is stable and correct, the horse can recognise and react to quite minor intentional variations in the seat contact. These seat aids can be very influential indeed, and a skilful rider will consider the seat the most important aid of all.

• *The driving seat, used correctly in conjunction with 'holding' hands, produces a steadying or collecting effect. This picture shows the energetic collection of an advanced horse performing piaffe.*

• *The driving seat used correctly, together with pressure from the legs and 'allowing' hands, produces extra forward movement. Here, the rider is asking for lengthened strides in trot.*

• *A fairly marked representation of the correct light seat – note that it is not a 'fork' seat, nor is the rider's upper body curled forwards.*

(b)

(a)

Positive seat aids

As with all the other aids, there is considerable variety in the *precise* ways in which the seat can be used. However, the following is a description of the main (fundamental) seat effects:

1. Rider's weight spread evenly over the buttocks and upper thighs – upper body normally erect. This represents the norm; the seat is 'in communication' with the horse, but not sending any specific signals.
2. More weight on the buttocks, less weight on the thighs, slight bracing of the lower back (the rider makes a little extra effort to sit up straight, moves the shoulder blades a little closer together and pushes the lower back *fractionally* forward). This is a 'driving' seat aid. Used together with pressure from the legs and with 'allowing' hands, it encourages extra forward movement. Used together with quiet legs and 'holding' hands, it produces a steadying, holding or collecting effect.[1]
3. Less weight on the buttocks, more weight on the thighs, upper body perhaps inclined (not curled) *very* slightly forward. This is a light seat, used to encourage a horse – perhaps a youngster or one who tends to hollow his back – to raise and 'swing' through his back.

[1] It is very important that this aid effect is used correctly and with discretion. Leaning back and driving hard with the seat will put the rider 'behind the movement' and may cause an inadvertent hardening of the rein contact. The horse will hollow his back away from the harsh aid, thereby blocking the action of his hindquarters; this hollowing and loss of activity will be exacerbated by his reaction to a restrictive rein.

• *Use of the seat and back aids. Rider (a) is sitting crooked at halt, with a collapsed right hip and a crooked spine. This crookedness is likely to affect the horse's way of going, as soon as he moves off. Rider (b) is performing half-pass left. Additional weighting on the rider's inside (left) seatbone, and pressure from the rider's right leg guide the horse to the left. However, when applied correctly, the seat aid does not result in the rider leaning to the left, nor does the leg aid entail the rider leaning to the right (which might happen if the rider tried to push too strongly). Thus we see the importance of correct posture: in the first case, the rider's faulty posture will have negative effects as soon as the horse moves; in the second case, the rider's good posture will assist the horse to perform a complex movement correctly.*

(a)

(b)

(c)

(d)

4. More weight on one buttock than the other. This is sometimes called a loaded seat aid; it should not involve the rider leaning sideways with the upper body, or collapsing the hip on the same side. As we have seen, a horse instinctively tends to rebalance himself underneath the rider's weight, so a rider may increase the weight effect of one side of the seat to encourage the horse to move under this weight. Such aids may be used in turns and lateral movements.

Negative seat effects

The effects described above are the benefits of a good seat. If the seat is incorrect and unstable, none of these things can happen with any consistency, but the horse will receive a succession of jumbled and largely unintentional messages through the rider's seat. Also, since an unstable seat will not provide a

- *Postural faults.*
(a) Tipping forward onto the fork. In this posture, the seat and back aids become ineffective, the lower leg is too far back and the rider may rest the hands on the wither for support, compromising the rein contact. If the horse were to stumble or spook, the rider would easily be dislodged.
(b) 'Foetal' posture. The back is curled forward, the tummy muscles are slack and there is no real weight in the seat. In this posture, the rider cannot ride 'leg into hand' or use the seat and back aids, either to push or hold the horse. On a keen horse in an exciting environment, the rider in this posture is almost certain to get carted.
(c) 'Behind the movement'. The rider is leaning back, and the lower leg is, consequentially, creeping forward. This can be the result of misusing the driving aid of the seat. Although it may induce more basic forward movement, it will not allow the horse to round his back and engage, so consequentially fast, flattened strides, rather than rounded, elastic ones result. It also has much in common with the old-fashioned 'hunting seat': on one level this may seem a secure posture for the rider over rough country, however, since it compromises the horse's ability to balance himself properly, it may not be so safe as it might seem.
(d) Trying too hard to get things right. A rigid, concave back, with tension in the arms. In motion, this rider will find it very difficult to absorb the horse's movement, or to keep her hands still.

shock-absorbing base of support for the rider's upper body, this will inevitably be bounced around by the horse's movement. Therefore, despite the rider's best efforts, it will be impossible to keep the hands steady, so all sorts of jumbled messages will be sent down the reins[2]. Furthermore, since bouncing around will make the rider feel insecure, there will be an instinctive tendency to grip the horse's sides with the legs (and possibly hang on with the reins). Harsh, gripping leg aids will tend to upset the horse and make him hurry (and thus even bouncier to sit on), and will also prevent the rider's legs from being free to send proper signals. The final scenario is a confused, upset horse, rushing around with no real direction from an increasingly unstable rider. The safest resolution to this situation occurs if the horse gives up mentally and becomes sufficiently inactive to allow the rider to scramble back into some semblance of a correct posture, from which they can blame the horse for 'being a nutter'.

It will be apparent from all this that a really bad or unestablished seat will make effective riding quite impossible. Indeed, it is axiomatic that newcomers to the sport should acquire the rudiments of correct seat and posture before they start trying to ride in the sense of exercising control over the horse. This is why reputable teaching establishments have traditionally introduced novices via the lunge or, at least, the leading rein.[3] However, it should be noted that even experienced, able riders can easily lapse into minor errors of seat and posture. While these may not have such devastating effects as those just described, they will still interfere significantly with effective riding and, to a certain extent, along the lines just mentioned (remember, the principles apply to everyone). It is, therefore, impossible to overestimate the importance of good posture. It is sound practice to check your posture (or have it checked by an experienced instructor) on a regular basis – and whenever you find yourself struggling for no apparent reason.

[2] This is why it is pointless for an instructor to tell a novice pupil with an unbalanced, insecure seat to 'keep your hands still'. It is impossible for the pupil to do this until the root cause of the problem is resolved.
[3] Nonetheless, depth, stability, feel and correct use of the seat inevitably take a considerable time to acquire. Novice riders should not be impatient in their efforts to influence the horse efficiently during this learning process, nor should they be impatient with the horse.

(a)

(b)

• *Inappropriate saddles for general flatwork. (a) A very forward-cut jumping saddle and (b) an old-fashioned showing saddle.*

THE SADDLE

If you find yourself struggling persistently to retain a correct posture, it may be worthwhile checking your saddle. It is very easy to blame the saddle, and it should be stressed that, in many cases, the rider is the only – or, at least, major culprit. However, a bad saddle, or one of inappropriate type, will make it very difficult to retain a correct posture for flatwork. Very forward-cut jumping saddles (including some which may be fine for their intended purpose) tend to draw the rider's legs and upper body forward, and some old-fashioned saddles throw the rider's weight too far back. You will also find it difficult to keep a correct posture in a saddle which is significantly too large or too small for you (although this may also be connected to the size of horse), and a saddle custom-built for one rider may prove anatomically unsuitable for another – especially if the riders arc of different sexes!

Two more thoughts on this topic. First, it is not essential to buy a dressage saddle for the early stages of training, even if you fully intend to ride the occasional lower-level test. A well-made general purpose saddle will prove quite adequate at this juncture; indeed, a rider who has not fully established a deep seat and long leg position may find some purpose-built dressage saddles quite difficult and uncomfortable to sit in. Second, the questions of comfort and fit are even more important to the horse than they are to the rider. A saddle that does not fit properly will inevitably, in one way or another, have an adverse effect upon the horse's way of going. Saddles, and horses, can change shape. If a horse begins to move in an uncharacteristically stiff, tense manner, it is worthwhile having the fit of the saddle checked by an expert. (If the saddle still fits properly, have the horse checked by your vet.)

The legs stay in communication with the horse by resting lightly against his sides (the Germans call this 'feeling the hair', which is a lovely and accurate description). They give specific aids by sliding along the horse's sides to the required spot and being applied, singly or in pairs, with varying degrees of pressure. Applied in tandem, they give signals to start movement. They are also used to maintain or increase forward movement but, while they are usually applied *in pairs* for these purposes, that does not mean that they are necessarily applied simultaneously or *in exactly the same way*. (We will look at these issues further in due course.) Applied individually, or with differing emphasis, they play a major role in producing and controlling sideways movement and changes of direction.

While educated legs remain quiet unless they have a specific signal to give, uneducated legs chatter and nag away mindlessly, sending no precise signals, but simply irritating the horse until, eventually, he becomes 'dead to the leg'. This does not mean that the nerves in his sides are destroyed (as can happen in a 'dead' mouth) but it means that the horse has become so fed up with trying to make sense of a stream of meaningless signals that he simply stops taking any notice of them.

As we have seen, negative leg aids can also be an involuntary result of bad posture. If, for example, the rider sits on the back of the saddle, the legs may be positioned too far forward to elicit forward movement from the horse. Gripping legs, often a result of postural insecurity, may also result from a rider's misconception about how to retain the horse's attention. In the latter context, they are the equivalent of thinking that you can only retain a person's attention if you grab them by the shoulder. There are subtler ways of doing this, which are less likely to cause resentment. We will examine such issues in due course.

THE LEGS

The rider's relatively long, strong legs naturally hang down against the horse's sides, providing the basis for sending signals by pressing against the horse. This pressure makes use of the horse's sensitivity to touch and his tendency to move away from physical pressure – a partly instinctive reaction which will be reinforced by training.

THE HANDS

We can now take it as read that our riding ancestors, mentioned earlier, determined that the mechanical link between the rider's hands and a sensitive part of the horse's head (his mouth), should be via reins and a bit (although some cultures did go with the rope and nose options). These mechanical links enable the rider to use manual dexterity to help guide and control the horse.

(a)

(b)

(c)

(d)

(e)

The hands meter out forward movement signalled by the rider's legs and seat: they allow forward movement by softening contact and, by quiet resistance, they form part of the aids to slow down, change gait downward, or halt. They also guide the horse's forehand in the required direction in unison with the leg and seat aids.

Good hands are quiet hands; their role is usually a supporting one. Unsteady hands (often the result of faulty posture) will confuse the horse; harsh, heavy hands will unsettle him, block (rather than control) forward movement, and create resistances.

Of course, hands can only act as aids when they are in communication with the horse – you cannot have a phone conversation if you and/or the other party have put the receiver down. In riding, 'being connected' is established quite literally by the reins and the bit. Basic contact occurs when there is just sufficient tension in the rein for both horse and rider to feel each other – this is pretty much the same sort of neutral communication as the rider's legs 'feeling the hair'. During the process of riding, many subtle variations of contact may be made, but the fundamental benchmark is that contact should be light but definite. One of the hallmarks of a thinking rider is the constant monitoring of contact – using the two-way communi-

• *Faulty leg positions.*
(a) Too far forward, with rider's weight on rear of buttocks. This posture makes correct use of legs, seat and back impossible. (It may be provoked or exaggerated by a badly made saddle.)
(b) Stirrup leathers too short for flatwork. It will be difficult for the rider to retain any depth of seat when the horse is in motion.
(c) Stirrup leathers too long – rider reaching for stirrups and perching on the saddle. (Gradual lengthening of the rider's leg position can be a consequence of increasing depth of seat but it is impossible to manufacture a deep seat simply by lengthening the leathers.)
(d) Slightly crooked – a little more weight on left hip, left foot slightly lower than right, left shoulder dropped a little.
(e) Feet too far home in the stirrups and toes turned out and down. This posture turns the insides of the rider's legs, which should be resting in contact with the horse, away from his sides. Subtle communication via the rider's legs will be impossible; aids will be given with the backs of the calves and the heels, and the rider's legs will swing and grip up.

cation to gain feedback. This monitoring may be of responses to subtle, intentional actions on the rider's part, or it may signal that something has definitely gone wrong. For example, if contact is suddenly lost, then either the rider has inadvertently given it away, or else the horse has either snatched the rein from the rider's hands or dropped 'behind the bit'. In all cases, action is required to re-establish the status quo. On the other hand, if the contact suddenly becomes harder, then either the rider has increased it inadvertently (perhaps by an involuntary loss of balance) or else the horse has increased it, either by his own loss of balance (falling onto the forehand) or by some act of resistance. Again, action is required.

At this point, we should look briefly at the horse's two evasions of coming 'above the bit' and dropping 'behind' it (explored more fully in Chapter 6). Although they appear very different, these actions have in common the fact that, by altering the carriage of his head and neck, the horse is trying to evade taking a proper contact with the bit. It is very important that these evasions are not accepted by the rider because they have been misinterpreted. The high head carriage of a horse who has come above the bit should not be confused with the concept of relative elevation of the forehand, which is often mentioned in connection with collection. Relative elevation comes about as a consequence of the collected horse engaging and lowering his hindquarters, not through him putting his head in the air (which will just stiffen his back and block the action of his hindquarters). Similarly, when a horse drops behind the bit, this should not be confused with him being light in hand. A horse who is truly light in hand is so because he is properly balanced: he is perfectly happy to take a constant contact on the bit, but this contact is light because he is not leaning on the rider's hands. A horse who drops behind the bit, however, is doing so for the express purpose of *avoiding* any contact with the rider's hands, which means that the rider has no communication with the horse's front end.

One basic point to bear in mind about contact is that what you can (or can't) feel in your hand will be mirrored by what the horse is feeling in his mouth. In fact, since the horse's sensation will be heightened, to some extent, by the action of the bit, we should take a brief look at this crucial piece of equipment.

(a)

(b)

(c)

(d)

BITS

Under British Dressage and British Eventing rules, all dressage tests at Preliminary and Novice Level, or the equivalent, must be ridden in a snaffle. The snaffle is the appropriate bit for training at these levels, and the permitted patterns are listed and illustrated in the British Dressage rule book. Provided that it is of the correct size, in good condition and suited to the shape of your horse's mouth, one of these permitted patterns will definitely be suitable for working your horse on the flat. By all means, take advice from an expert saddler or instructor in this respect, but do not be tempted to experiment with weird and wonderful bits (especially ones that you can't compete in), or keep chopping and changing in the hope that a slightly different pattern will solve some major schooling problem. In a book originally published in 1658, the Duke of Newcastle wrote:

Neither is it a good bridle that breaks the horse well. For if they were made tractable by this piece of iron put in their mouths, the bit-makers would be the best horsemen in the world…The bridle, I confess, is of some use, tho' but little; art avails much more, as all your excellent riders know…it is not the bridle, but the art of the rider, that renders the horse tractable.

That was true then, has been true throughout the intervening centuries, and remains true today.

An ill-fitting, damaged bit will ruin your horse's schooling; the most suitable, comfortable bit will assist you in schooling to best effect, but no bit ever made will school your horse for you, or cancel out major defects in training.

- *Faulty uses of the hands.*
(a) Tight, short hold of the horse's head, restricting forward movement.
(b) No rein contact (rider's posture is also encouraging the horse to go in a hollow outline).
(c) Hands resting on horse's withers, interfering with rein contact (note also rider's straight arms and the angle between bit and rider's elbow).
(d) Hands not level (many riders who are, themselves, 'one-sided', tend to hold their dominant hand higher than the other one).

THE VOICE

It is undeniable that the *tone* of a rider's voice can be used to soothe, encourage or tell off a horse, and that horses can be trained to respond to simple specific commands (as when lungeing). However, although the voice is universally acknowledged to be a natural aid, its use in dressage competitions is prohibited, any use being penalised by deduction of marks. Whatever you may feel about the logic of this, it is the rule. Therefore, while the voice can be used constructively in moderation when training at home, anyone who intends to compete is advised not to rely on it too much, nor to allow the horse to come to *expect* voice aids.

ARTIFICIAL AIDS

Down through the ages, riders (usually the less skilful ones) have experimented with all sorts of devices intended to reinforce the natural aids. Most of these have had more to do with forcing the horse into responding than with educating him to do so. Nowadays, most of the more barbaric devices have been abandoned and the majority of existing artificial aids and gadgets are invariably auxiliary reins in some form or another, the most undeservedly popular being draw reins. Although some legitimate uses are claimed for these devices, they are most commonly used by riders seeking non-existent short cuts, generally to the considerable detriment of the horse. They are rightly prohibited both during dressage competitions and whilst warming up for them.

The two artificial aids which have remained generally acceptable and which are allowed in most (although not *all* – check!) dressage competitions are the whip[4] and spurs. At first sight, this may seem ridiculous and, if you were to think in terms of beating or stabbing the horse into submission, it would be. Correctly used, however, both have legitimate roles to play in supporting and emphasising the leg aids.

[4] The whip, for example, is not allowed in the dressage phase of horse trials run under British Eventing rules.

THE WHIP

The whip, applied just behind, and at the same time as, the leg, can help when schooling or reschooling a horse to respond to the leg aid. From a training point of view, this makes much more sense than resorting to ever stronger leg aids, which would be exactly the opposite of what is desired. The whip can also be used to 'call to attention' a horse who has become preoccupied with whatever is going on outside the arena, rather than paying attention to what he should be doing inside it. Sparing and subtle use of this kind, either during training or during an actual dressage test is quite legitimate – we are not talking here of beating the horse up, but of a quick smack that says 'Oi, pay attention'. Although riders are often reluctant to use the whip during a test, a judge will almost certainly prefer its intelligent use to a rider's indulgence in heavy and improper 'natural' aids.

SPURS

Spurs have schooling and reschooling functions similar to those of the whip, and they may also be used in the remedial training of a horse who has learnt to lean on the rider's leg (for example, cutting in round corners or ignoring leg aids to move sideways). Since spurs amplify the effect of the leg aids, they can also be used to give very quiet, subtle, but effective aids. In fact, when worn by skilled riders engaged in advanced training, this is their main use.

• *Correct and incorrect use of the whip. Rider (a) is using the whip in a way that allows her to soften her rein contact and allow the horse to go more forward in response to the aid. The way in which rider (b) is using the whip has increased the rein contact, so the horse is getting conflicting signals (see also text on The Principles of Applying the Aids).*

(a)   (b)

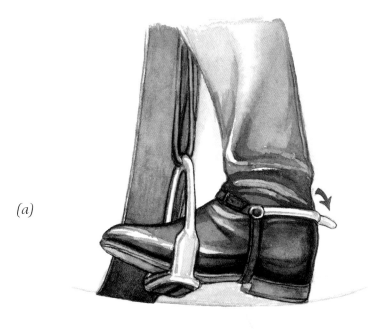

(a)

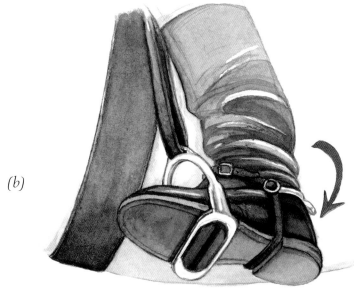

(b)

• *Correct and incorrect use of the spur.*
(a) A slight inward flexion of the rider's leg produces an effect which heightens the leg aid.
(b) Turning the heel inward and kicking will startle, and perhaps bruise, the horse. Riders must not use spurs until they have established a correct, controlled leg position.

Some riders are reluctant in principle to wear spurs, because they have a mental picture of spiky and barbaric devices – but modern spurs, of the sort permitted under dressage rules, are nothing of the sort.

Other riders are reluctant to wear them because they believe that wearing them inevitably means using them. This, however, is not the case provided that they are properly fitted and the rider's basic leg position is sound. A rider who discovers that wearing and using spurs amounts to the same thing will be quite right to remove them, but the main lesson to be drawn from this is that the rider needs to pay urgent attention to overall posture, since this can only happen to a rider who habitually grips the horse's sides with the backs of the calves and heels.

It is, of course, the case that artificial aids should be used sparingly. When they are used in a schooling or reschooling role, they should become less and less necessary if the schooling is effective. If they are required as a matter of course to reinforce requests for forward movement, then there is something wrong either with the horse or with the rider's other aids.

THE PRINCIPLES OF APPLYING THE AIDS

We have seen that the aids are the rider's means of communicating with the horse – 'speaking' to him, through physical signals, in a way he can understand. Although people and horses are very different, there are some principles of human communication from which we can learn valuable lessons in communicating with the horse.

In human communication, we use recognised words to express our thoughts. When communicating with the horse, each single aid represents a word. If we were to write, accidentally, 'ggo' and 'stp', it is probable that someone with a reasonable grasp of English would guess that we meant 'go' and 'stop'. Similarly, an attentive horse with good basic training would probably 'guess' the meaning of an imprecise aid, but he would have to think about it, might be unsure, and would be slow to respond. What, however would he make of the aid equivalent of 'gsotpo'? The answer of course, is that he would just be confused. The lesson to be learnt from this is that, since we want the best possible response from the horse, we must 'check our spelling' – the individual aids should be precise, and they must certainly make sense.

Although, in human communication, a single word is sometimes sufficient to convey our meaning, this is fairly rare. Usually, a sentence is necessary or preferable to make our meaning clear. Again, the same principle applies when communicating with a horse; we often need to combine several aids to make up a 'sentence'. Fortunately, because the horse is a fairly simple creature and we are asking him to do fairly simple things, our 'sentences' can also be quite simple.

Nevertheless, it is still important that we 'construct our sentences' properly. The first thing this entails is choosing the right 'words' (aids). In human speech, it is simply confusing to use a word which is perfectly correct in itself, but does not mean what you intend to say. There is no point in saying 'now' if you mean 'soon', or 'stop' if you mean 'slow down'. Furthermore, there is no point in blaming the listener for doing what you said rather than what you meant – and the same applies to the horse.

When constructing sentences it is also necessary to put the words into the right order. If we say to someone 'get dressed and get out of bed', we may *intend* them to get up, then put their clothes on, but what we are actually *telling* them to do is to lie in bed struggling into their clothes and then get up. This may or may not be easy or desirable from their point of view, but it is not our *intention*. An example of this sort of thing in riding is the rider who asks a stationary horse to turn by pulling on one rein, and *then* asks him to move forwards. It would have been correct 'sentence construction' – and vastly easier for the horse – to have asked for the forward movement *first*.

So, how do we decide upon our 'sentence construction' when applying the aids? In speech and writing, there are grammatical guidelines – so is there an equestrian equivalent? The answer is yes, and it relates to the basic purpose of the aids, which is to encourage active forward movement (or the desire to move forwards) and to adjust it according to our requirements. From this we can learn, when constructing our 'aid sentences', to give priority of order and/or intensity to the aid involving forward movement. Our 'aid sentences' should communicate to the horse along these lines:

'Please go forwards/into canter/thank you'.
'Please keep going forwards/but change down a gait/into trot/thank you'.
'Please go forwards/and round onto this circle'.

Making the forwards aid the key does not mean that the other aids should be applied one at a time 'by numbers', like some old-fashioned army drill. They should, in fact, be applied in a harmonious way so that they reinforce and confirm each other – which is what the technical side of good riding is all about. However, this is only possible if we, as riders, are clear in our own minds about what we want from the horse, and what he has to do in order to deliver it. These are issues that we will explore further in due course, when we are discussing specific movements and figures. For the moment, if we continue the analogy between person to person and person to horse communication, we can learn some further lessons which will be of use to us as positive, considerate trainers.

- *Coordinated and uncoordinated aids.*
(a) Uncoordinated transition from trot to walk. Rider's hand acts too strongly; leg is passive. Horse hollows away from the strong rein aid, then more or less collapses into walk.
(b) Coordinated transition from trot to walk. The rider's leg acts sufficiently to say 'please keep going forward', while the deepened seat and containing hand say 'but change down a gait', producing a smooth transition into an active walk.
(c) Uncoordinated transition from walk to trot. The rider's legs drive the horse forward, but her upper body and hands resist, causing the horse to perform an uncomfortable transition into a necessarily hollow outline.
(d) Coordinated transition from walk to trot. The rider's legs ask or the upward transition and her hands allow a soft, forward transition into a rounded outline.

(a)

(b)

(c)

(d)

These are:

Don't 'shout'. Human beings shout at each other because they are angry, because they think it will somehow make their unclear meaning clearer, or because they are just vacuously noisy. While there may be rare occasions when we are justified in being angry with the horse (if he shows clear and flagrant disobedience), anger is never justified in cases where the horse simply does not understand, or cannot obey. Giving harsher aids to a horse who does not understand them is like shouting at a foreigner who is struggling with the rudiments of your language. Giving harsher aids to a horse who cannot obey (physically cannot do what you are asking) is like sounding your horn at the driver of a car whose rear axle has snapped. Such behaviour is far more damning of the perpetrator than the recipient. It sends out the signal 'I am stupid and boorish'. In a similar vein, it is inappropriate for a rider to be simply 'loud', to give strong aids for no obvious reason. Aids should always be as light *as is effective* and one result of correct training is that the aids become gradually lighter while remaining effective, as the horse learns to recognise them more readily.

Don't nag. Aids should be specific signals which last only as long as is necessary. Once the horse is doing what is asked of him it is pointless – in fact confusing – to keep asking him to do it. If you were to ask someone else to make the tea, and they went into the kitchen, put the kettle on and started to sort out the cups, there would be no point in your continually shouting 'Make the tea, make the tea'. The other person would probably resent it, and it wouldn't get the job done quicker – it would be much better to keep silent, or call out 'thanks'. Similarly, we thank the horse, once he has obeyed, by ceasing or easing the aids.

Don't be arrogant. Arrogant people 'tell' others, but they don't listen and, if their instructions are garbled and imprecise, any misinterpretation is always 'the other person's fault'. Such attitudes do not represent real communication, and they are hopeless in the context of training horses. Proper communication is a two-way process: you should always 'listen' to what the horse's responses are 'telling' you. If the horse readily does what he was asked, and does it well, you can assume that your own aids were fully understood. Do not just take this as read – view it as positive evidence that *you* are doing something right (which won't always be the case). If, however, the horse does not respond as required, you must be prepared to 'listen' to what the horse's reactions are 'saying'. Is the horse being wilfully disobedient? Does he not understand? Is he physically unable to obey? Were your aids so jumbled that the horse just could not interpret them? If you wish to play an active, positive role in training any horse, you *must* be prepared to ask such questions. Learning to answer them correctly is part of the *art* of riding.

Finally, on this subject, we should consider the matter of consistency. It is often stated that, to avoid confusing the horse, and to get a consistent response, the aids themselves must be consistent. This is true, but it must be understood in context. The truth about the basic need for consistency can be easily demonstrated. For example, over the years, there have been many combinations of aids devised and used to make a transition to canter. If you were to study these, then go into the school and ask for repeated canter transitions, using each different set of aids in turn, it would be no surprise if the horse became confused, despite the fact that each sets of aids *can* (for better or worse) induce canter. Similarly, if your horse currently does a reasonable transition from walk to trot in response to a moderate squeeze from your legs, it would be pointless to ask for trot on one occasion by giving him a mighty boot in the ribs, and the very next time by giving an almost imperceptible aid that hardly compressed his coat.

Thus, consistency *is* very important. This does not mean, however, that *exactly the same* combination of aids (what we might call 'absolute consistency') will always produce the same quality of response in different horses or even, in the long term, in the same horse. In the first instance, this is because horses vary in conformation, sensitivity and speed of reaction. Therefore, although the *principles* upon which the aids are based will remain consistent, the *precise* way in which they are applied may have to be modified slightly from horse to horse, in order to produce the best response. (To make an analogy, if you are a driver, think about the subtle modifications you have to make if you drive someone else's car – even if it is quite similar to your own. If such modifications are necessary when dealing with something mechanical, it is hardly surprising that they will be required when dealing with living creatures.)

The state of an individual horse's education is also a factor, since this will affect both his level of understanding and his physical ability to respond to the aids. Again, we can make a direct comparison with human learning. If you were teaching someone how to tack up for the first time, you would have to explain every detail slowly and carefully, then give them the chance to have a go. (In effect, you would be saying 'I want you to tack up a horse – don't worry, I'll show you what to do'.) The first few times they did it themselves, you would have to watch and correct any errors; for some while after that, you would still check what they had done. However, once you were confident in their ability, you could simply ask 'Will you tack up my horse please?' The point is, while the basic process (tacking up) and the underlying principles (the need to ensure that everything fits correctly and is secure) remain unaltered, the 'aids' have been refined from detailed assistance to a simple request. This refinement is the acid test of how the rider's aids are being applied throughout the training process. You must remain basically consistent in what you ask for but, as the horse's physical and mental abilities improve, it should become easier for him to recognise and respond to your requests. In other words, you will not need to 'explain' everything to him quite so plainly, or in quite so much detail, so you should find that you are gradually getting a better response to lighter aids. If the opposite seems to be the case, this is strong evidence that something is wrong, either with your aids, or with the horse himself.

However, while a desire to refine the aids is always admirable, it must be seen in the context of steady progression. It is important to remember that all aids are communications, and effective communication requires reference to what the horse you are riding understands and can do *now*. Thus, the secret of giving good aids is to find the lightest combination that will produce the correct response[5] *from this horse at this stage of training.*

[5] Use of the term 'correct response' rules out any possibility that unnecessarily harsh or fundamentally incorrect aids can be used, since any response they may produce will not be correct.

·3·

THE IIORSE

As we have seen, 'dressage' simply means 'training' and, since all ridden horses are being trained they are all, in that respect, dressage horses. The common supposition that one needs an idealised horse in order to 'do dressage' is therefore untrue. Of course, in terms of competitive dressage, there is no doubt that a horse of excellent conformation and temperament has a considerable natural advantage – but this principle applies to any discipline. A bold, careful 17 hh horse who can jump 6 ft has a considcrable advantage as a showjumper over a 15 hh cob, but this does not mean that the cob might not prove very successful at his appropriate level. By definition, very few horses will be capable of *excelling* in any field, but this is no reason why they should not be trained to perform to the best of their and their riders' abilities – and a decision to pursue this goal may bring unexpected rewards.

The one problem with horses who combine excellent conformation and temperament is that they are rather rare, and tend to be very expensive. While any rider will naturally try to obtain the best and most suitable horse available, few can find, or afford, perfection. For most of us, the best hope is to find a horse who, despite various faults and failings, has certain characteristics which suit our own personality and purposes reasonably well. Since (if we are sensible) we want to *enjoy* riding and handling our horse, we will tend to be quite heavily influenced in our choice by temperament. This is eminently sensible, so long as we do not go too far overboard in ignoring physical flaws, and so long as we remain mindful of those flaws we have accepted as a trade-off for getting an affordable horse who will be our 'pal'.

As we shall see later (Chapter Five), there is no denying that faults of conformation affect the mechanical efficiency of the horse, and it is obvious that temperament cannot directly have a positive influence upon this. As a general rule, however, a rider can achieve more with a horse of imperfect conformation if that horse has a particularly good temperament. If the horse is by nature cooperative and eager to please, he will usually try his best and, *provided that he is ridden considerately,* he will not turn requests to do things he finds difficult into grounds for active resistance, as a nervous or sullen horse might do. (The emphasis here on considerate riding is of fundamental importance. There is a vast difference between asking a horse, gradually and diplomatically, to do something he finds initially difficult with the long-term aim of making it easier for him, and suddenly demanding that he do something that he finds almost impossible and probably painful. The latter is simply a cynical abuse of the horse's good nature, and will swiftly destroy the relationship between horse and rider.)

Provided that their flaws in conformation are not major, good-natured but physically imperfect horses are generally easier to deal with than those of better conformation but suspect temperament. This is because, even when they are handled with

• *Horses and ponies come in different shapes and sizes. Even those without obvious conformation defects will show differences in their natural movement and their outlook on life. Examples here are (a) common, crossbred type, (b) Connemara, (c) Hanoverian, (d) Cob, (e) Thoroughbred.*

(a)

(b)

(c)

(d)

(e)

tact, skill and determination, there is always a chance that the character flaws in the latter will prevent them from achieving their full potential. It is noteworthy that, across the range of disciplines, even the most skilled riders are frequently frustrated and exasperated by brilliant but temperamental performers. The average rider, therefore, should be very wary about getting involved with a horse whose good looks are not reflected by his personality.

You should certainly exercise great caution in respect of a horse who has serious behavioural problems. It may be tempting to get involved if, for example, he is a very well-made individual and you believe that his behaviour has been caused by bad handling or riding rather than being a natural characteristic. Certainly, bad behaviour is *caused* more often than it is inbred but even so, once it exists, you need to be very sure of your abilities before you attempt to eradicate it. Even then, dealing with such problems rarely comes under the heading of 'enjoyment', and is best left to those experts who are paid to do so.

Another type of horse to avoid is one who has a condition likely to cause recurring unsoundness. We are not talking here of relatively minor faults of conformation, but of major, existing conditions. We have known of people taking on such horses 'because he seems so nice'. But however cheap such a horse may be (even if he is free!), and whatever excellent qualities he may possess, he will, through no fault of his own, cause the training process to be frustratingly interrupted, and there is a high probability that all will end in heartbreak.

There is one other point that we would like to make here, and that concerns total unsuitability. Owners quite rightly get very attached to their horses and, despite their mutual foibles and odd moments of exasperation, they are usually determined to work through their problems and make progress. Indeed, recognition of this fact was one of the main reasons for writing this book. Just occasionally, however, it happens that someone acquires a horse who proves to be totally unsuitable. It may be that the owner is frightened of the horse, or it may be that the horse has very little natural aptitude for the rider's main area of interest. When this happens, it is better all round for the rider to sell the horse and acquire another one. In such cases (especially if the rider felt that they somehow could not handle the horse)

there is inevitably a sense of defeat but, in reality, the decision usually proves beneficial to both horse and rider. There is a difference between a situation that requires determination and tenacity, and one that is truly a lost cause.

These considerations aside, there is no reason why every owner should not try to do the very best with the horse they have. In riding, it is very rare indeed to have even a chance of obtaining perfection. Usually, the aim must be to go as far as possible towards realising the horse's full potential and the sense of achievement comes from knowing that you are at least heading down the right road. Never forget that, by the very act of riding, you are inevitably training your horse – so why not give it your best shot?

PRE-CONDITIONS FOR TRAINING

In order that a horse can be trained in a constructive way, several pre-conditions must be met. He must be healthy, sound and have a reasonable amount of energy. These matters may seem very obvious, but it is amazing how often they are ignored.

HEALTH

Although few people would attempt to train a horse who was really ill, there are many who try to proceed while the horse is not properly well. They may argue 'I can't take time off every time I get a cold, so why should the horse?' or 'It won't do any harm just to work quietly'. Well, depending upon the circumstances, the horse may not suffer any further damage to his health, but it is unlikely that the overall effect upon his training will be positive. A look at two common examples will show why:

1. If a horse has some mild virus, his energy level will be reduced, and it will be reduced further if he is (as he should be) on a 'resting ration'. As we have seen, the fundamental requirement for training is that the horse must have a desire to go forwards; if his physical energy is reduced (and he is also not feeling very well), this desire will be diminished. This means that all his work will be sub-standard, and the rider may be tempted to use stronger driving aids than would normally be necessary – two retrograde steps.

2. If a horse has a mild cough or throat infection (which often involves swollen glands), he will be uncomfortable and resistant if forced to flex and work on the bit. His head carriage will be unsteady, and he will generally be more comfortable going with his head nearly on the ground. This, coupled with a reduction in impulsion, will tend to put him on the forehand. Attempts by the rider to remedy this will probably result in the horse resisting both leg and hand – hardly a recipe for progress.

It should be obvious, then, that trying to improve a horse's schooling under such circumstances is, at best, a waste of time. If there are grounds for exercising a horse who is not properly healthy under saddle, the best course of action is a gentle hack, walking on a long rein.

SOUNDNESS

Trying to school a horse who has gone lame is pointless, and likely to make things worse. Apart from the moral issue of working a horse who is, at best, uncomfortable, gait quality will inevitably be impaired. The horse will not go straight in any movement, because he will be trying to avoid loading the affected limb. As a result, he will place extra weight on the opposing limb (which is why a lame horse will 'nod' on the sound forelimb in trot) and, if work is continued over a long period, this extra stress can cause problems in the hitherto sound limb.

It should be stressed that we are talking here about actual unsoundness, as opposed to muscular stiffness, or other conditions which a vet has advised should be 'ridden through'. However, where such conditions exist, remember that the initial work must be done *with the sole purpose of alleviating them*. Furthermore, the work that follows should take account of the fact that the horse had such a condition to begin with.

ENERGY

The work demands made of a horse must be matched by his energy level. Feeding is an art and science which horse owners should study in some detail; suffice it to say here that you cannot expect good, active work from a horse who lacks energy, and that it is dangerous for both horse and rider to pump a horse's

energy level up significantly beyond the demands made upon it. Both sluggishness and bad behaviour can be caused by incorrect feeding; neither will help the training process and, in both cases, the horse must be considered victim, not villain.

FITNESS

The question of fitness is related to both energy levels and to the overall training programme. One major function of training is to improve fitness, but this must take place gradually, it will not occur if demands are made which the horse's system is unable to meet. If a horse is unfit, over-stressing his system will make setbacks (often of a serious nature) very likely, and will also provoke gait irregularities. In a fat horse, the danger is of damage to heart, lungs, joints and tendons. Excess fat may limit the action of the limbs so that, if the horse is pressured into more forward movement, he will necessarily respond by taking short, scuttling steps. If a horse is in poor condition, this really needs to be properly investigated and improved before he is asked to work at all. Working a 'poor' horse will cause further loss of condition, and provoke gait irregularities arising from lack of strength and balance; forging, brushing and plaiting.

Therefore, before a really unfit horse can be asked to do any actual work, his condition must be improved. With a fat horse, this must be achieved by short, regular periods of walking for two weeks or so, followed by at least three weeks during which the exercise period is gradually increased, and includes increasing periods of *steady* trot. The same process is also suitable for a previously 'poor' horse, once his initial condition has been improved.

There are four points which cannot be over-emphasised when discussing fitness:

1. You cannot make a horse fit simply by feeding high-energy food. Instead, you will provoke metabolic disorders and behavioural problems.

2. You cannot gallop a horse fit. Working an unfit horse fast will over-stress tendons, muscles, heart and lungs, with the risk of major breakdown. If the horse is in poor condition, further loss of condition will occur.

3. You cannot hurry the fittening process. Building muscle, hardening tendons and increasing heart and lung capacity all take a certain time. The horse's organs and tissues cannot and will not develop more quickly than Nature intended.

4. *Regular, progressive exercise* is the key. You cannot get a horse fit by leaving him in his box all week and going out for four-hour hacks at the weekend; this regime will just make him stiff and invite a whole host of problems.

(a)

(b)

(c)

• *Horses in (a) gross, (b) poor and (c) good condition. Fast work should only be introduced in the latter stages of the fittening process.*

·4·

FIRST THOUGHTS ON TRAINING

The purposes of training are to educate the horse – to make him more aware of what is required of him – and to improve him physically, so that he is able to perform a greater variety of work more easily and in better style. (Further to this, we would repeat the point made in the Introduction that much of the work performed within a proper training programme has its own intrinsic value. While riders preparing to compete may focus on improving movements and exercises so as to perform them better in the test arena, they can overlook the fact that the simple act of doing them along correct lines is assisting the horse's overall training. For example, the most important aspect of a correctly ridden circle is not that it will gain you a good mark in a dressage test, but that it constitutes a valuable gymnastic exercise for the horse. Later on, we will look at the various gaits, transitions, movements and figures that appear in tests up to Novice Level more fully in this light.)

It is a general principle that the more he is able to enjoy his training, the better a horse's progress is likely to be – practical reasons for this being that a happy horse is more likely to offer active forward movement and exhibit the signs of willing submission.

Horses, like people, respond best to a training system which is sympathetic towards their weaknesses (while seeking to strengthen them) and which recognises, rewards and builds upon their successes. The general method of training must be consistent, logical and progressive and – as discussed earlier – it is essential that the teacher communicates in a language which the pupil understands.

In order for progress to be made, the training programme must introduce a steady stream of new ideas. This does not necessarily mean only work which is completely new to the horse – it includes new, better ways of doing things which the horse already does regularly (an example might be improving the horse's existing rhythm and balance in trot). It should be noted that doing 'new work' of this sort can sometimes be *harder* than introducing a completely new idea, because it involves changing existing bad habits (re-schooling).

The introduction of new work will sometimes stretch or test the horse a little, mentally and/or physically. This is a necessary part of training but, in order to keep the horse confident and willing to please, it is important not to overdo it, whether by making demands which are too frequent, too prolonged, or too great. Instead, new ideas and exercises should be introduced along the following lines:

1. Before work on new ideas is started, the horse must be in a receptive condition – physically warmed up and mentally attentive.
2. Each must be a next step in a logical sequence of training. You cannot go into the school and decide, out of the blue, to try a new movement which is unrelated to the work the horse has performed previously with success. It would, for example, be very foolish to decide, on a whim, to attempt rein-back on a horse who could not already do a good, correct halt.
3. New ideas should be introduced one at a time and not in too quick succession; the horse must be given time to allow them to sink in. Similarly, when introducing a 'big' new idea – a

wholly new movement, for instance – you should, so far as possible, break it down into individual phases. Building towards a goal in this manner will produce far better (and quicker) results than trying to get there in one quantum leap.

4. Work on a new idea should be fairly intense, but it should be done for only short periods at a time, and these must be interspersed with work which the horse finds relatively easy and pleasant. It is also useful for the alternative work to provide some sort of contrasting balance: if the new work has been on rein-back, then alternative work might be an active working trot: if the new work has been lengthened strides in trot, then the alternative work might be large circles at walk.

Introducing new ideas along such lines will offer the best chance of success but, if a period of new work does not produce the desired result the alternative, easy, work will act as a cooling-off period, during which you and the horse can 'unwind' and re-establish harmony, and you can give calm consideration to what went wrong. It is a mistake, in such circumstances, to 'hammer away' fruitlessly and without a re-think, with horse and rider becoming increasingly upset by each other. Regardless of 'who was right and who was wrong', nothing positive will be achieved and the horse will simply come to think of the new work as unwelcome and unpleasant.

However, if it is fruitless to 'hammer away' when things go wrong, it is just as foolish to do so when they go well. This can happen if a rider becomes over-excited by success, or has thoughts of consolidating a new idea through prolonged repetition. Apart from being unnecessary (the horse has a good memory, and once an idea has sunk in, it will not be readily forgotten), this creates the risk of the horse becoming bored, tired or stale, and success being turned into failure. Rather than going down this path, you should think of the alternative work as a reward for the horse; the successful new work can be consolidated by further short sessions over a period of time.

From the above, it should be clear that a correct training programme cannot be tied to a rigid timescale. Although it is necessary to map out what you want to achieve in general terms, it is neither necessary nor sensible to start work on new movement just because you have reached a certain date on the calendar.

The time to start new work is when the horse has shown himself ready and, indeed, many good trainers attribute their success to a willingness to 'let the horse tell them' – and this may be either earlier or later than they themselves anticipated.

By 'letting the horse tell them', such trainers are demonstrating rapport and empathy with the horse, but this is not as mysterious as it may sound. It is simply an extension of communicating with the horse, along the lines discussed in applying the aids. If you wish to get on well with your family and friends, you cannot just take them for granted and tell them what you want – instead, you have to consider their feelings and points of view, and you sometimes have to negotiate and compromise. If you want a big favour from someone, or if you want to persuade them to take a big step, you try to pick your moment; a time when they are in a good mood and likely to be receptive to your suggestion or request. It is the same with a horse; the time to move on to something new is when he is 'full of beans', going confidently about his work with ears pricked, and almost saying 'Okay, what shall we do next?'

Since this is most likely to happen in the absence of problems, let us look next at the types of problem which may arise in training; how to define them and how best to avoid, or solve, them.

PROBLEMS IN PRINCIPLE: CAUSES AND CURES

In order to deal with problems, it is first necessary to define precisely what they are. Failure to do so can lead to an incorrect or inappropriate response, which may make things worse. A horse undergoing training may exhibit the following responses.

LACK OF UNDERSTANDING
The horse quite simply does not understand what is being asked of him. This is without doubt an indication that the rider is trying to go too fast with the horse's education. Whether or not the horse is 'stupid' is irrelevant; if he does not understand, he does not understand. The rider must exercise patience, concentrating upon going ahead in the smallest possible stages, and rewarding any glimmer of understanding on the horse's part.

CONFUSION

While not altogether dissimilar from the above, this describes a situation where the horse would be capable of doing what was required, if he could interpret the rider's request. The rider is not being clear or consistent enough with the aids. The solution is to apply the aids more clearly, not more forcibly.

FEAR

This can be divided into fear of pain and instinctive fear. If a horse is reluctant to do something because it is hurting, or is going to hurt him, then the source of pain must be removed. Unusual reluctance to do something, coupled with signs of tension, often indicates pain, whether from undiagnosed illness or lameness, or from ill-fitting tack. Obviously, attempting to school a horse who is in pain is bound to prove counterproductive, and says little for the sensitivity or intelligence of the rider.

Instinctive fear will make a horse tense and have adverse effects upon his submissiveness – in severe cases, upon his basic obedience. As with lack of understanding, judgements about the horse's lack of boldness are (at least in the short term), irrelevant – if he is frightened, he is frightened. Instinctive fear must be dealt with slowly, because it is deeply ingrained. If a horse is genuinely frightened – of cows, tractors, fairground noises or whatever – he will not work well in close proximity to such objects until the fear has been properly eradicated. This requires a long-term mixture of firmness and sympathy on the rider's part – short-term, forceful methods will just serve to *reinforce* the fear.

DIFFICULTY

Mental difficulty relates mainly to lack of understanding and confusion. Physical difficulty occurs when the horse understands what is required, but his lack of strength, suppleness or balance, or the limitations of his conformation, make it hard for him to obey. Although lack of balance may be caused by the conditions of the moment (including bad riding!), the other causes require long-term attention. In the case of limitations imposed by *skeletal* conformation it is probable that the rider will have to make permanent compromises with the 'ideal' (examples of this will be examined in the next chapter).

It is important to learn to assess the *degree* to which movements are difficult for a horse. In order to make physical progress, a horse must, to a certain extent, be asked to do things which stretch his physical capabilities a little. This is exactly the same as a human athlete building up a training regime – once he can run ten miles quite comfortably, he asks his body to do an extra mile or so. What the wise athlete does not do is jump from running five miles to fifteen; he wants to build his body up, not break it down and exhaust it. Similarly, with a horse, the wise rider keeps the final goal in mind and is satisfied with a little more each time.

A horse who is asked to do just a *little* more than is really comfortable may show a minor degree of resistance, but this is just equine nature, in the same way as it would be human nature for someone on a fitness programme to ask 'Have I really *got* to do three more sit-ups?'. The point is that the person really *can* do three more sit-ups, and the rider's attitude in an equivalent case should be 'Come on, you can do it', chivvying the horse along kindly without making a major issue of it.

Making unreasonable physical demands of a horse is an altogether different matter. Apart from the risk of causing physical damage it will *inevitably* cause serious resistance. Although this resistance may be partly mental (the horse saying 'I really can't manage this'), it will be mainly physical, arising from muscles or joints which simply *cannot* act as required. If, for example, a horse has developed strong muscles underneath his neck and has virtually no muscle along his crest, it will be physically impossible for him to work straightaway in a correct outline for any length of time; what is required is a programme which will *gradually* alter the distribution of the muscle. Attempting to force a quick change of outline by prolonged use of draw reins or similar would simply be a pointless abuse.

ANTICIPATION

This is when a horse tries to do something before he has been asked to. Anticipation is not the same as disobedience – indeed, it shows a basic willingness on the horse's part. It comes about because the horse starts to associate something other than the rider's specific aids as being the signal to perform a movement. *If it becomes ingrained, this is the fault of the rider, not the horse, and punishment is never justifiable.* A rider may, for example, always ask for a transition at the same place in the school or, out hacking, always shorten the reins before cantering. In the first instance, it is hardly surprising if the horse starts to *offer* the transition at the marker and, in the second, it is hardly surprising if the horse starts to think of an increased rein contact as the *signal* for canter.

In the early stages of teaching new work, a *little* repetition of set up can be helpful while the horse is getting the hang of things. However, the first signs of anticipation are a signal that the penny has dropped, and that it is time to start doing this work at different times and places.

DISOBEDIENCE

It is particularly important that we define what is meant by disobedience. To punish a horse who is confused, frightened or finding something difficult is the height of folly. Not only is it unjust, but it will also cause the horse to add unpleasantness to his other associations with the situation (that is, he will not just think 'this is confusing' or 'this is difficult', but rather 'this is confusing and unpleasant' or 'difficult and unpleasant').

True disobedience is when a horse refuses to do something of which he is known to be fully capable, or does something which he knows to be contrary to the rider's wishes, at a time when there is no reasonable excuse for his actions. True disobedience is fairly rare – much rarer than many riders believe – and it must be stressed that *uncharacteristic* disobedience is often the first sign of pain or illness. That said, true disobedience does sometimes occur; a horse may be simply lazy, self-indulgent or bad tempered. In many cases, disobedience is related to inherited temperament (it will be noted that a certain horse will tend to exhibit a certain *type* of disobedience), but this can be made worse by bad or ineffective handling and riding.

Bearing in mind that all riding is training, the rider must take steps to discourage any disobedience the moment it occurs. A horse is a big, strong animal, and riders who consistently allow horses to get away with disobedient acts are simply and inevitably storing up trouble for themselves – or someone else. The longer real disobedience goes uncorrected, the more ingrained and blatant it will become, and the process of eradicating it will become longer, more difficult, and may require harsher methods.

Of course, reaction to an individual act of disobedience must be in relation to the act itself. A fair-minded rider will not wish to punish a horse more harshly than he deserves, and to do so will simply help sour their relationship. If the disobedience is quite minor, then a scolding voice, a firmer-than-usual (but not improper) aid, or a quick smack may suffice. Indeed, if the rider is alert in such cases, and nips minor disobediences in the bud, then it may be possible, by such mild measures, to prevent the problem from developing any further.

This, certainly, should be the aim, because serious disobedience is quite a different matter. We have already noted the inadvisability of taking on a horse who has major behavioural problems but, if you find you have done this, you must decide from the outset whether it is worthwhile trying to resolve them, and whether you have the skill, strength and resolution to do so. Although it is unpleasant to dwell on such matters, it is a fact that dealing with such horses can be difficult and dangerous and, as with all training, the rider's efforts will not leave the horse unchanged – they will either cure him or make him even worse.

Before leaving this discussion of problems, let us consider what Brigadier Kurt Albrecht, former Commander of the Spanish Riding School, has to say on the subject:

Most of the cases of resistance or even open rebellion by the horse are founded upon that most human of all human attributes, which is to forgive one's own weaknesses and to be intolerant of the weaknesses of others.

Kurt Albrecht *Principles of Dressage*

To put it another way, when your horse does a movement badly, you should consider at least the *possibility* that you may have had something to do with this. It is a general principle that (subject to their physical limitations) horses go as well or as badly as they are ridden. Horses have no moral sense – they are incapable of feeling an obligation to do their best 'against the odds'. Certainly, they can show willingness and enthusiasm for work they enjoy, but they will soon down tools if it is made difficult or unpleasant for them. A wise rider will treasure and encourage the former reaction, and seek, so far as possible, to guard against the latter.

·5·

HOW CONFORMATION CAN AFFECT TRAINING

Conformation is a big subject; there are very many ways in which imperfect conformation can affect a horse's way of going and ultimate potential. Keen students can find many books which will improve their knowledge of this topic, and it is not the intention of this book to discuss it in great detail. However, since few of us have access to perfect equine specimens, it is very important to be aware of some of the most common aspects of skeletal conformation which will influence a horse's ability to move correctly and respond to the basic controlling aids.

Although it will be a bonus if the information given in this chapter dissuades you from acquiring a horse with more significant flaws, the aim is not to completely rule out from training a horse who exhibits them, but to point out why it may be difficult for him to do certain things, so that you may be persuaded to work with and around these difficulties, rather than blaming the horse unjustly for being cussed, and making demands which induce resistances and loss of confidence. The more serious the defect, the more important it is to observe this principle. The best results will be obtained in such cases by acknowledging the defect fully, and being content to improve the horse so far as is practicable. Ignoring the defect and riding the horse as if he were a perfect specimen is futile, and almost certain to result in regression rather than progression.

THE HEAD

Because the horse's head is a main contact point for the rider, its size, shape and the way in which it joins the horse's body are all factors that can influence communication and training.

Head set on high. Skeletally, this is a consequence of how the occipital bone (at the back of the skull) joins the atlas (the first cervical vertebra). If the occipital sits abnormally high on the atlas, this will cause a noticeable tendency for the horse to carry his head high and poke his nose, even when loose. It is physically impossible for such a horse to flex correctly at the poll to the same extent as a horse with a well-set-on head, so the rider must be satisfied with less. If excessive efforts are made to 'get his head down', such a horse can only respond by overbending through his neck, still without full flexion at the poll. Then, in addition to being not fully 'in hand', he is also likely to be on the forehand, so one problem will have been made into two.

Head set on low. Skeletally, this is the opposite of the above, and makes the horse excessively flexible at the poll. The rider will need to encourage active forward movement and maintain a light rein contact, otherwise the horse will soon learn to tuck his nose behind the vertical, greatly limiting control. *It is very important that riders of such horses do not encourage them to go in*

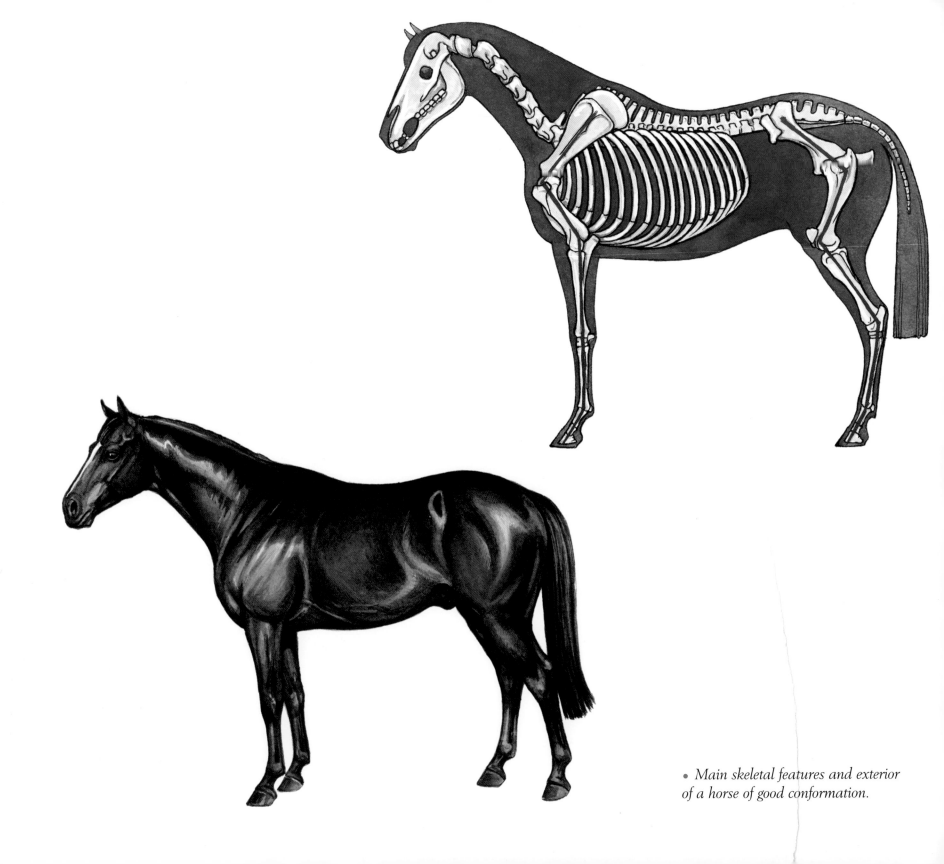

• *Main skeletal features and exterior of a horse of good conformation.*

this fashion, in the mistaken assumption that they are on the bit. This carriage of head and neck, in which the horse is not seeking the bit, but dropping 'behind' it, is the antithesis of what is required.

Large, heavy head. A large, heavy head is an extra weight out in front for the horse to balance, and it will tend to put him on his forehand. If such a horse can persuade his rider to help carry some of this weight in his hands, he will probably do so. The rider must, therefore, avoid being conned in this way and should encourage the horse to bring his hind legs well forward underneath him, to assist him in carrying and balancing himself. We will discuss this in more detail in the next chapter under Lack of Balance.

(a)

(b)

(c)

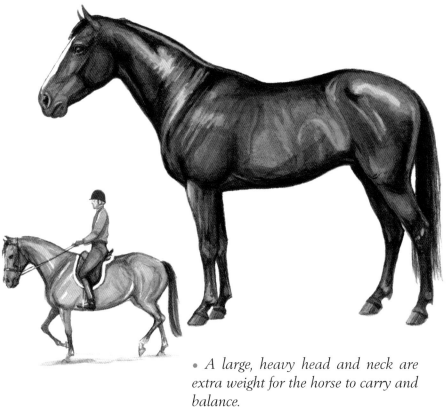

• *A large, heavy head and neck are extra weight for the horse to carry and balance.*

• *The way in which the horse's head is set on to his neck will have an impact upon his natural head carriage. (a) Set on well; (b) set on high; (c) set on low.*

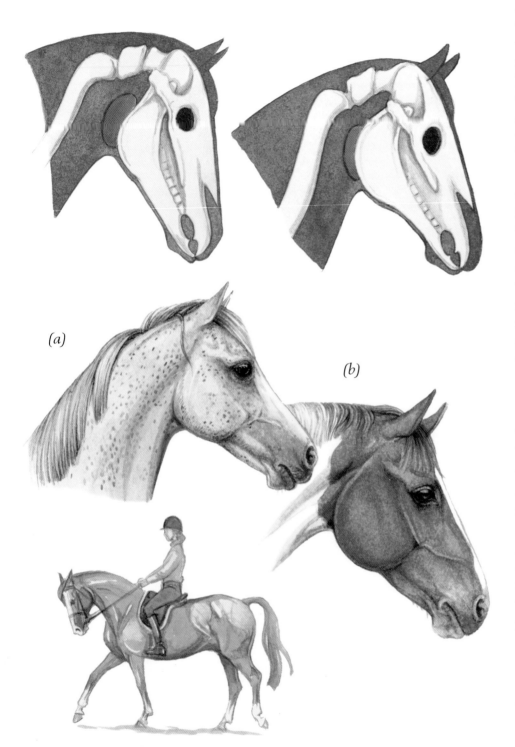

(a)

(b)

Relationship between lower jaw and neck. The relationship of the width of the space between the lower jawbones to the thickness of the neck behind them is most important. There must be room for the jawbones to clear the neck when the horse flexes at the poll, otherwise the ends of the jawbones will compress the parotid (salivary) glands to a painful degree. This, understandably, will make the horse reluctant to flex, so he will probably try to evade requests to do so by bending through the whole of his neck, becoming too 'deep' in front and perhaps behind the bit. This problem of conformation is often associated with cobby types, whose necks are too thick to allow clearance by the jawbones, but the effect may also occur in horses with abnormally narrow spaces between the jaws. Although the root cause is different, such horses share a fundamental problem with those whose head is set on high. Since it is physically difficult (if not impossible) for them to flex to a normal degree, the rider must necessarily be prepared to accept less. Asking for more than the horse can give will not solve the problem, it will just generate additional ones.

THE NECK

The neck is an important feature in terms of the horse's balance and the rider's control. We have already seen that the way it joins the head can be very significant, but its shape and its junction with the shoulder region are also important.

Ewe neck. The most difficult type of neck to deal with is a skeletally created ewe neck. The ewe neck shape created by incorrect muscular development (big muscles underneath the neck, no muscle on the topline, head in the air) is a product of bad riding, and can be corrected in time by

• *Adequate room for the jawbones to 'clear' the neck (a) allows the horse to flex at the poll in comfort. If the ends of the jawbone compress the parotid glands (b) the horse will be reluctant to flex at the poll, and may overbend through the neck instead.*

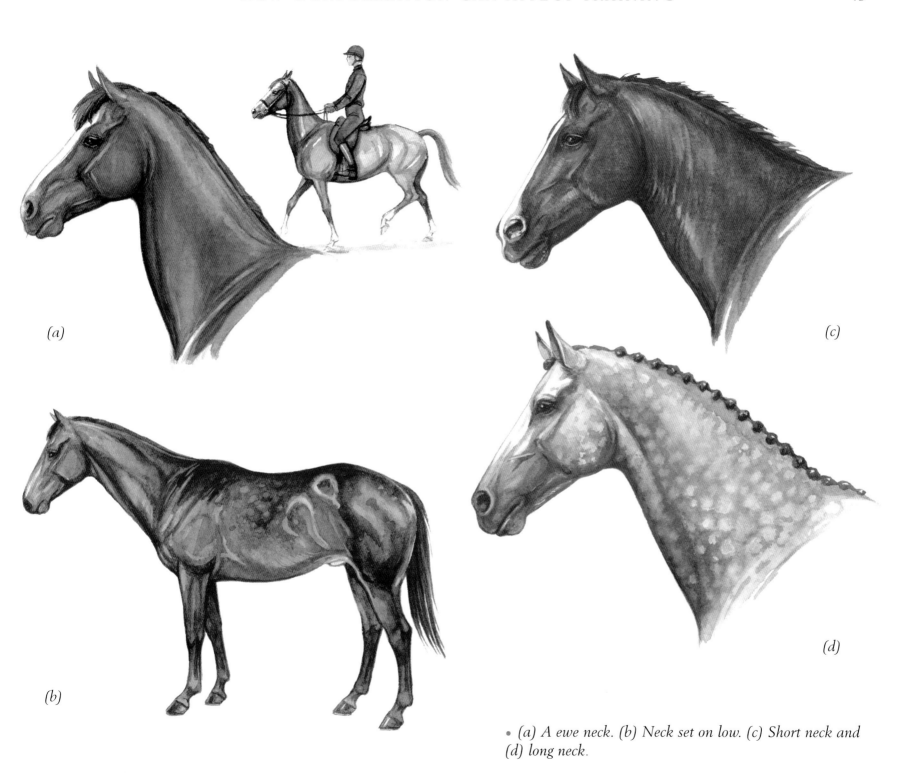

• (a) A ewe neck. (b) Neck set on low. (c) Short neck and (d) long neck.

remedial schooling. However, a ewe neck resulting from skeletal conformation is a different matter, especially (as is often the case) if it is associated with a head set on high and a skeletally hollow back. There is no denying that such conformation is a considerable disadvantage for both horse and rider but, faced with such a challenge, one thing is certain: a horse built like this will find it physically impossible to respond to efforts to pull him into a rounded outline with draw reins or similar devices, and any attempt to do this will inevitably create major resistances and very probably cause serious damage to the vertebrae. Less coercive, but determined efforts to 'get his head down' with excessive rein effects may well result in the horse's head being lowered, but still without real flexion at the poll, and still with a concave neck. Such a posture will place the horse firmly on the forehand and lock up any connection along his topline – a sort of riding equivalent of putting the horse in a 'full nelson'.

Whatever progress is made with such horses will be the result of patience and diplomacy. This means that lesser demands are made of the horse, but that he is expected to be obedient to these lesser demands. The hardest thing to accept is that the degree to which such a horse can really be ridden between leg and hand (and thus encouraged to engage and round his topline) will inevitably be compromised by his conformation. Trying too hard to obtain benefits usually associated with impulsion may create problems with submission (because the horse can't do what is required) and impair the gaits (because the horse may be compelled into running or scuttling along). Thus the best course of action is to try to ensure that the horse is properly responsive to light aids, so he is at least *obedient* to the leg and hand, and can be ridden between them to the extent of his ability, without sacrificing such natural rhythm as he may possess.

Set on low. A neck which is set on low will emerge from the horse's shoulder lower than normal. Mechanically, it will tend to place more of the horse's weight on his forehand, and it will certainly make it easier for the horse to lean on the rider's hand, if he is so inclined. If such a neck is accompanied by a large, heavy head, the horse will be naturally on the forehand to a significant degree. (See Lack of Balance in Chapter 6.)

Length of neck. Ideally, the length of neck should be in proportion to the rest of the horse. Long or short necks do not, of themselves, pose any great difficulties, but they do provide their owners with greater opportunity to evade incorrect use of the aids. Long-necked horses are particularly adept at evading (sometimes by over-reaction) attempts to steer them primarily with the reins. A short neck, which is structurally strong, can assist its owner (should he so choose) to 'set' his head and neck and 'tank off' – usually a reaction to hard hands and a weak seat. Alternatively, such a horse may overbend through his neck, tuck his head in and run off whilst behind the bit – probably in response to being driven into unyielding hands. It must be stressed that, while such reactions are *facilitated* by conformation, they are not inevitable *consequences* of conformation, but manifestations of inappropriate riding.

THE SHOULDERS

The shape of a horse's shoulders and withers has a great influence upon his ease of movement, and how comfortable he is to ride. The ideal is a well-sloped shoulder with fairly well-defined but not over-prominent withers, which taper gently into the back. If such conformation is matched by well-formed hindquarters, the horse will cover the ground well, and be able to extend his stride readily. On the other hand, straight (upright) shoulders will give the horse a rather short, choppy action in front[1], which is less comfortable for the rider, makes lengthening the stride more difficult and less marked, and places greater stresses on the lower forelegs.

A major conformation fault in some horses is that they have big, powerful shoulders which are not matched by the hindquarters. This can occur in cross-bred horses who have not come out as an overall blend of both parents, but as 'half-and-half'. Left to his own devices, such a horse will naturally use his powerful shoulders to supplement the action of his weak hindquarters in providing locomotion, thus putting himself

---

[1] A straight shoulder is not the *only* factor that contributes to such an action. Short, upright pasterns, and being 'tied-in' at the elbow (little space between elbow and ribcage) may also contribute.

determinedly on the forehand. The problem is made worse if the horse is also long-backed.

Because he is doing what is natural for him, it can be a difficult, long-term process persuading such a horse to engage his hindquarters. First, it is necessary to muscle up the hindquarters as much as possible so that, in the horse's terms, they are worth engaging. This is best done by a lot of steady trotting uphill but, inevitably, such a horse will try to run up the hill using his shoulders. Therefore, with this, and all other work, the rider will have an almost continual need to use half-halts (with relatively quiet legs) to try to encourage the horse to take more weight on his hindquarters. The uses of half-halts are explained in the next chapter.

THE BACK

As with the neck, a length of back that is in proportion to the horse is to be favoured overall. There are various pros and cons associated with shorter and longer backs.

Short back. A reasonably short back is quite desirable in terms of strength, balance, and assisting the horse to go 'united'. However, while a short back is strong, it will tend to be somewhat stiff both longitudinally and laterally. The shorter the back, the more marked this stiffness may be. Since a short back is likely to give a rather bouncy ride, the rider must make every effort to develop a deep, absorbent seat, so that gains in balance arising from conformation are not forfeited by the rider's involuntary movements. Any lateral stiffness will make it relatively difficult for the horse to bend correctly on turns and circles, so he will need to do plenty of exercises aimed at improving suppleness.

• *The effect upon movement and stride length of sloping shoulders (bay) and upright shoulders (grey).*

Long back. A long back may be comfortable to sit on, and more flexible than a short back, it will also be structurally weaker. Especially if such a back is also rather hollow, the horse will be able to carry less weight than other features of his conformation might suggest.

A long-backed horse will not be able to move his hind legs as relatively far underneath his body as a horse with a shorter back, so the degree of engagement of his hind limbs will be relatively less, and it will be harder for him to balance himself and achieve

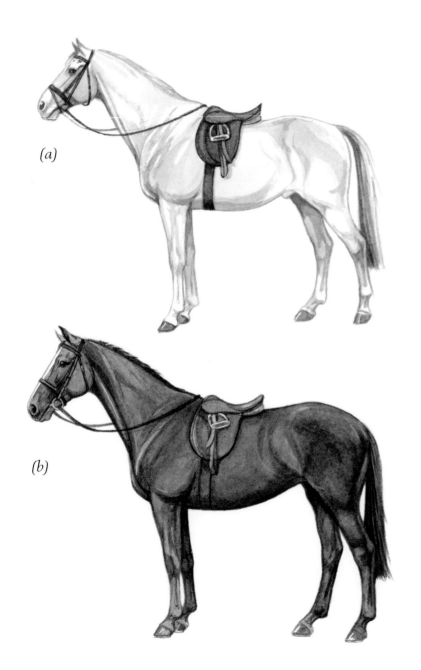

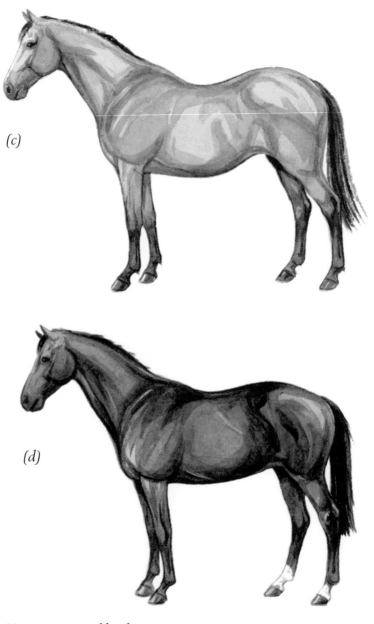

• *Various types of back:*
(a) short back, (b) long back, (c)dipped back, (d) roach back.

lightness. A long back will accentuate the effects of certain other faults such as heavy shoulders, poor hindquarters and trailing hind legs.

Back abnormalities. This description is used to cover such conformation as dipped backs and 'roach' (markedly convex) backs. Given the desirability of a rounded outline, one might readily think that the latter was markedly to be preferred but, in practice, this is usually not the case. A dipped back is, without doubt, a weak structure but, given a relatively light and considerate rider, dip-backed horses often perform surprisingly well. On the other hand, while the roach back is a very strong structure, it is also a very rigid one, and roach-backed horses find it hard to move with any fluidity. Therefore, the rider of such a horse must be careful not to make demands based upon misconceptions about the 'rounded' back.

Horses with these abnormalities require exceptional care in the choice and fitting of a saddle.

THE HINDQUARTERS AND HIND LIMBS

The hindquarters and hind limbs are the 'powerhouse' of the horse: an arrangement of jointed levers which use the horse's energy to propel him forwards. Any defect in this area is bound to have some adverse effect upon the quality of movement. If the defect involves incorrect articulation of any joint, it will also place increased stress (and wear) on that joint and on the associated tendons, muscles and ligaments. Unfortunately, there are many possible faults in this area which can affect a horse's straightness, power or potential for remaining sound – these can be studied in books specifically about conformation. Two faults which have obvious effects upon basic forward movement are:

Croup-high. Although it is an advantage for the croup to be well formed and muscle-covered, some horses have a very pronounced croup, higher than the withers, associated with disproportionately long hind legs. These horses tend to take long,

● *The effect upon movement of the horse being croup-high (grey) and having hocks trailing (Appaloosa).*

but rather hurried steps and lack of fitness (especially lack of muscle in the quarters) will often have an adverse effect upon rhythm and cadence (correct timing and sequence of footfall) at all gaits; they are especially prone to overreaching.

Despite the long steps, this conformation tends to tip extra weight and stress onto the forehand, and the natural carriage of head and neck will be long and low, with the horse leaning on the rider's hands if allowed to. This conformation makes it difficult for the horse to take his weight back onto the hindquarters and achieve lightness.

When a horse built like this is trotting, the action of the hind limbs is such that the rider may have the sensation of being kicked up the backside at every stride, and it is also rather difficult to absorb the horse's motion at canter. The rider of such a horse must therefore pay especial attention to quality of seat. Also, such a horse must never be bustled, since this will simply worsen any deficiencies in rhythm and balance. Instead, the best policy is to ride as quietly as possible, indeed to try to slow the naturally hurried rhythm a little, so that the horse has more time to balance himself and 'get out of his own way'. (It is not unusual for young horses, who grow in spurts, to appear intermittently croup-high. In such cases, the horse's growth may well even out with maturity. Where the condition is seen in mature horses, however, it will be skeletally established.)

Trailing hocks. (A simple way to assess this is to look at the hind limbs when the horse is halted square. With good conformation, a vertical line down from the point of buttock should run pretty much straight down the back of the hind cannon bones. Trailing hocks will place the hind cannons significantly further back.)

If a horse's hocks are 'out behind him', it is very difficult or him to balance himself, carry himself or propel himself powerfully forward. Especially when associated with a long back, this defect makes it particularly difficult for a horse to canter; his instinct will be to run faster and faster in trot. Canter work with such horses should initially be in a straight line, and preferably slightly uphill, to shorten the stride and improve the chance of some degree of engagement. As a general principle, the horse's natural canter, which is likely to be long and lollopy, should be accepted in the early stages. Improvement is most likely to occur as the horse's balance and musculature improve gradually; attempts to force it against the limitations of conformation will probably destroy whatever gait quality there is. Early attempts to shorten the canter through a strong rein contact will literally prevent such a horse from cantering at all.

It will be noted from this brief summary that a horse will not necessarily have one fault of conformation. He may be less than perfect in several respects, in which case it will be necessary to take them all into account when deciding how best to ride him. Hopefully, he will also have various good points, which will make some aspects of training more straightforward. As we said earlier, one of the best characteristics of a horse with moderate conformation is good temperament. If you have this on your side, cherish it – it is your most valuable asset.

·6·

TRAINING FLAWS – CAUSES AND CORRECTIONS

We have seen that flaws in conformation can be a cause of imperfections in movement and that, when this is the case, any efforts to improve the situation must take account of the flaw which caused it. However, horses can move incorrectly for reasons that are unrelated, or only partly related, to conformation; the main one being incorrect riding. We should, therefore, look at some of the more common training flaws, to see how they can be avoided or rectified but, before doing so, we should consider the matter of the horse's outline.

THE QUESTION OF OUTLINE

The horse's general outline, and the way in which he moves within it, are major indicators of whether or not he is being trained along correct lines. Unfortunately, many people become obsessed with outline without understanding why it is important, or what correct outline involves, and this can lead to major errors in training.

One of the major aims of training a horse is to move his point of balance (centre of gravity) backwards, more nearly beneath that of the rider, so that the horse can carry both himself and the rider with minimum effort and to maximum effect. To help achieve this, correct training increases the strength and suppleness of the horse's hindquarters and back. This enables him to engage his hind limbs more effectively beneath his body, so that they can play a greater role both in supporting and balancing him and in propelling him powerfully forward. The more able a horse becomes to engage his

hind limbs, the more weight he will carry on them. In consequence, the hindquarters will tend to lower, and his back will round upward.

Another aim of correct training is to encourage the horse to be sensitive to the actions of the rider's hands, and to flex at the poll.[1] It is, however, very important that he does this as an act of acceptance (going willingly forward into the rider's hands and yielding to them) and that he does not simply overbend through his whole neck as a means of escaping the actions of the hands. The latter makes it very difficult to control the horse, and it is also obvious that there is a world of difference between a horse evading an aid and his willing acceptance which, as we saw earlier, is a sign of true submission.

Taken together, the developing ability of the horse to engage his hindquarters and his willingness to accept the hand are the essence of his coming on the aids. However, as these processes continue, the most obvious effect is, for many people, the change in the horse's topline. The extent to which this has changed will depend upon the horse's stage of training, his conformation and the skill of his rider but, in a fully trained horse performing collected work, the topline will look *very* rounded, especially in comparison to an untrained or poorly trained animal. Also, the most instantly eye-catching features

---

[1] This is not simply a case of the hands controlling the front end and the legs controlling the back end in isolation. The horse has a major ligament – the supraspinous ligament – that attaches to both the poll and sacrum (part of the pelvis). Therefore, a rider who has the horse truly between leg and hand has control of both ends of what, in effect, is a giant elastic band joining the two ends of the horse

- *Training flaws may be more or less obvious. Horse (a) initially looks to be going quite well, but he is forging (see left lateral feet). Horse (b) is falling into trot, his hocks are trailing and he is very inactive. Horse (c) is stiff in his back and above the bit. Horse (d) is showing some lack of balance on a circle.*

• Equine outlines.
(a) Young horse in early training under saddle.
(b) Training well under way; the horse shows an improved natural outline, with more engagement.
(c) Advanced horse performing collected work.

of such a horse may be the rounded curvature of his neck and the angle at which he carries his head, and it is these features which lead some people into a fundamental misunderstanding. Whereas they are, in fact, *consequences* of correct training, they are often interpreted as being a precondition for it ('I've got to get my horse's head down so I can start doing dressage'), or even as being the essence – the whole purpose – of training.

It is these misinterpretations which can lead to a destructive obsession with the horse's front end, with the rider trying to force or 'fiddle' the horse's head down whilst showing scant regard for what is (or is not) going on behind the saddle. The *least* destructive consequence of such action is that the horse will go 'too deep in front' and show insufficient activity in his hind limbs. Depending upon circumstances, and what gadgets may be employed in the process, worse possibilities include causing back or neck problems, creating serious resistances and producing a horse who either shuffles around like some hapless prisoner in medieval shackles or learns the bizarre trick of running away with his head in his chest.

None of these consequences is remotely desirable or necessary. If you ride your horse actively forward into sensitive hands which gently 'ask' to be accepted and remain still when the horse complies, you will be taking the first steps towards improving the horse's outline *in conjunction with his way of going*. As with all aspects of training, the correct development of the horse's outline will necessarily be a gradual process. Note that the requirement, in Novice Level tests, is simply that the horse 'maintains balance and rhythm *and a natural rounded outline, without restriction*'. A more universal adherence to the principles behind this concept would undoubtedly prevent or lessen many of the problems which arise when horses are being trained. However, let us now go on to look at some other specific flaws in training.

HORSE INACTIVE

Symptoms
Rhythm too slow and laboured, horse not showing any signs of engagement; not tracking up in working gaits.

Causes and cures
Lack of energy resulting from illness, incorrect feeding, unfitness; pain from undiagnosed lameness. Cease schooling until condition remedied.

Staleness/boredom caused by lack of variety in work. Introduce variety; note whether horse perks up.

Unfamiliarity with school work. Some horses, for example those who have only ever hunted or raced, may not, at first, understand the change of regime to working in an arena. They have always been stimulated into activity by going across country in company, and find working alone in the school confusing and boring. Introduce short periods of school work on returning from invigorating riding in the open – or ask for some simple school movements straight after a good canter whilst out. If restricted to the school, warm up briefly, then, if he jumps, stimulate the horse with a little straightforward jumping *before* your main work on the flat.

Selective idleness. Some horses are reluctant to exert themselves unless it suits them. This type will plod reluctantly out to the heath, then try to run away, and will stride out in determined fashion on the way home if it happens to be nearing lunchtime. In other words, they have plenty of energy, but expend it on their own terms. This is sheer disobedience, and must be nipped in the bud before it develops into serious resistances. When dealing with such horses, you must be determined and able to impose your will on them, otherwise they will impose theirs on you. Do not make the mistake of nagging away with your legs on such a horse – he will simply ignore you. Instead, he must be asked once, politely and correctly, to show more activity and, if he does not obey immediately, the next request must be reinforced with a sharp smack of the whip behind your leg. You should continue to demand an *immediate* increase in activity every time the horse even hints at idleness until he ceases to do so. Hopefully, you will be able to use the whip and other aids more lightly as the message sinks in.

Any concentrated period of work aimed at curing selective idleness should be done in trot, the gait in which the horse can

• If a healthy horse is plodding along through sheer idleness, do not work harder than him – use your whip correctly to wake him up and send him about his business.

most easily show reasonable activity and maintain his balance. This will minimise any problems resulting from his attempting to evade work by adopting *too fast* a rhythm (see next training flaw). Always try to avoid making the horse hurry in walk and canter.

RHYTHM TOO FAST

Symptoms
The horse takes short, hurried steps, rather than longer, measured ones. This may also (especially at walk) affect his cadence – see below.

Causes and cures
Nervous tension in the horse. This may result from incorrect diet or discomfort (badly fitting tack, etc.), in which cases locate the cause and remedy it. It may also be seen in a horse who has just come to a new yard, or is placed in another novel situation, in which case no great demands should be made until he has had time to adjust. (Note that there is no aid that can *make* a horse relax – he can only be encouraged and allowed to do so. This is why, for example, young horses must be given time to acclimatise to a showground environment before they can be expected to perform.)

Nervous tension in the rider. The rider may be a little nervous of the horse, or of the situation in which they are riding. It is very difficult for a rider to completely conceal such tension, and any that the horse perceives will almost certainly cause tension in him. However, if the rider can relax a little (the old remedy of deep, steady breaths can be useful), this relaxation should also be reflected in the horse. Depending on circumstances, businesslike attention to some basic but simple work (such as simple figures in rising trot, concentrating on rhythm, softness and accuracy) may be beneficial to both horse and rider.

Rider bustling the horse out of his natural rhythm. It is all too easy to for a rider to make the horse 'run away from the leg' when trying to obtain more engagement or more activity. The horse usually does this in response to nagging or clamped-on legs.

As we saw in Chapter 2 (The Principles of Applying the Aids), repeated nagging is rarely effective. The rider should give distinct, meaningful aids. If the horse does not respond to these, the next step is not to produce a kind of screaming repetition, but simply to ask *why*. We will consider this further, with respect to engagement, in Lack of Balance. So far as general lack of activity is concerned, we have just looked at this, and seen some solutions which are likely to be more constructive than an endless drumming away at the horse's sides.

There is one scenario which might, in some respects, be considered an exception to this. A hurried rhythm may be a temporary by-product of dealing with the selective idleness described above. In this case, the horse may be hurrying as a form of evasion (he thinks that if he responds to the rider's demands by 'running away' briefly, the rider will stop trying to make him work harder), or else he is just trying a simple con to avoid a forthcoming slap with the whip. Although hurried rhythm is never desirable it is, in these circumstances, a secondary problem – the rider's task is first to ensure a greater degree of general activity and *then* to concentrate upon improving the quality of movement. If a horse has been hurrying solely as an evasion, the sooner his underlying idleness is cured, the less chance there is of the hurried rhythm becoming ingrained. Furthermore, so long as there is no other cause, there is no reason why the horse should not work in a better rhythm once he has been convinced that he has *got* to work.

POOR CADENCE

Symptoms

Cadence is a term that is used by different people to mean slightly different things. Its root is the Latin word *cado* (fall) and we are using it in the context of footfall. Thus, poor cadence means that a gait is not performed in its correct 'time' (measured sequence of footfall). For example walk time should be 1.2.3.4, in regular sequence. If a horse hurries in walk, he will tend towards moving his legs in lateral pairs, so that the sequence will become 1.2–3.4. Other examples of poor cadence are forging in trot and cantering in four-time, or disunited.

• *Running, hurried steps, and the benefits of improving the rhythm.*

Causes and cures

Poor cadence can be caused by undiagnosed physical problems or conformation flaws, but other common causes are:

Weakness/tiredness/ lack of fitness. The horse will move better when he is stronger/rested/ fitter.

Rider error. Rider either bustling the horse, or allowing him to run or, alternatively, trying to hold an over-exuberant horse mainly with the hands. The remedy, in the first case, is to ride more quietly. Both the running and the over-exuberant horse should be dealt with by the rider sitting quietly but deep and relying mainly on seat and back rather than harsh hands to contain the movement.

LACK OF BALANCE

Symptoms

Poor rhythm and cadence, running into upward transitions and falling into downward transitions, leaning in or out on turns and circles.

Causes and cures

Weakness/unfitness. The simple answer is to make the horse fitter and stronger. This will produce very obvious benefits in a horse who was basically in quite poor condition. However, since a correct, ongoing training programme will *continue* to improve the horse's fitness and strength, it should have a *continual* effect upon his capacity to balance himself. (This is why advanced movements, requiring true collection can only be performed by fit, strong horses.)

Riding errors such as described under Poor Cadence, and inappropriate aids. Avoid errors; give more thought to how the aids are applied.

Poor rider posture unbalancing the horse. Work to improve posture, especially stillness, depth of seat and the straightening of any natural crookedness (good lunge lessons will help).

[2] A brief glance at a horse will show that he is not naturally symmetrical, front to rear, but has a relatively large head and neck 'stuck on' the front.

Faults of conformation which place the horse on the forehand (examples given in the previous chapter). Try to remedy or work with such defects so far as is practical.

ENGAGEMENT

As we have seen, there are specific faults of conformation that increase the extent to which a horse goes on the forehand. However, there is also a natural tendency[2] for most horses to carry more weight on the forehand than is desirable, and this is the single and most universal cause of lack of balance. As we saw in Chapter 1 (Impulsion), reducing this tendency is one of the main aims of training. The essence of doing this is to persuade the horse to engage his hind limbs, so that they step more underneath his body mass and carry some of the weight that had previously been supported by his forehand. As he learns to do this, he will gradually adjust his balance from a state in which it is tipped forward (on the forehand) to a state in which weight is pretty much evenly distributed over all four limbs. If training is further advanced along correct lines, the horse will achieve a state in which he is carrying more of his weight on his hindquarters, which is the essence of collection. For our purposes, however, a state of equilibrium can be considered a significant advance – so how is the necessary level of engagement achieved?

The basic requirement of engagement is a positive stepping forward of the horse's hind legs, an action that will be stimulated by the rider's own leg aids – but these have to be employed discreetly. If the horse is being asked to 'step under' more, he must be *allowed* (given time) to do so. Nagging, bustling aids do not encourage bigger, more active steps – they provoke short, scuttling ones, which are exactly the opposite of what is required. It can be useful, therefore, to think of the aids as reflecting the response wanted from the horse – they should be steady, measured, and given in time with the movement of the horse's hind legs. As the horse responds by engaging more, there will be a sensation of additional movement beneath the rider's seat and a lightening of the rein contact resulting from the horse's improved balance.

When asked, however correctly, for more engagement, some horses may be reluctant to comply. Such horses may be inherently lazy – in which case they will need 'waking up' before being asked to exert themselves. However, this lack of response is more frequent in horses who, because of their conformation and/or past training, have become confirmed in moving on the forehand. When asked to engage more, such horses will respond either by leaning more determinedly on the bit or trying to run 'through' it (sometimes called 'running out of the front door'). The rider's ability to deal with such evasions depends largely upon correctness of posture. If the seat is weak and the upper body curled forward, the rider will tend to be pulled forward, placing more weight on the horse's forehand and making the situation worse. Any attempt to raise the forehand by pulling on the reins will result in a tug of war and, although the horse will win, it will not add to his desire to show active forward movement. What is required, instead, is a deep seat and a strong, erect upper body, acting in effect like a powerful lever. A horse who tries to lean or pull against this will find it a very different proposition from the hands of a rider who is more or less in a foetal position. Gradually, it will dawn on him that, if the rider is not prepared to carry him, he had better start carrying himself.

Once again, we emphasise the word 'gradually'. If a horse has become confirmed in moving on the forehand (and especially if there are significant conformational reasons for his doing so), it may take him some time to adjust physically and mentally to a new way of going. Also, we would emphasise that adopting a posture which prevents the horse from pulling on *you* is not at all the same thing as you pulling on the horse. What is being described is the mechanical advantage of a correct, upright posture. What is *not* being advocated is leaning back and pulling on the reins. Apart from anything else, this would drive the horse into a hollow outline and make engagement impossible.

THE HALF-HALT

Increasing engagement is then, the basic remedy for lack of longitudinal balance. There is, however, another valuable tool available to the rider who needs a *momentary* improvement in balance – for example, just before riding a transition or when beginning a turn. This tool, which is also useful for increasing the horse's attention, is the half-halt.

The half-halt is an interplay of the seat, leg and rein aids, these aids being used with slightly different degrees of intensity depending upon circumstances. It is an action that can seem rather esoteric and mystifying, and it has to be said that a good deal of feel is involved in its application. But this is its essence – and the essence of effective riding in general. Subtle but effective half-halts can only be applied by a rider who has the horse on the aids *and who is 'listening', through these aids, to the horse's movement.* ('Can I feel active movement through my seat? Is the horse answering my leg? Has the rein contact changed because the horse has changed his balance or rhythm?') This is the two-way communication we mentioned in Chapter 2, which lies at the core of proactive riding. The tuned-in rider, who has the horse on the aids and is continually receptive to feedback, will be able to respond to minor changes in the horse's balance or attention in a way that is almost pre-emptive. In other words a minor, subtle but immediate action will resolve an incipient loss of balance before it really becomes apparent to an observer. (The principle behind this pre-emptive correction applies to many other aspects of riding, for example the correction of momentary crookedness. Again, it is a skill that is acquired gradually, through experience.)

So, how is the half-halt actually achieved? As we have seen, it involves an interplay of the aids but, reduced to its basic elements, it works like this. The tuned-in rider senses, for example, a slight loss of balance in the horse – perhaps he has quickened his rhythm and fallen a little onto the forehand. The rider responds by slightly increasing the driving effect of the seat (see Positive Seat Aids, Chapter 2) and the leg aids, which constitute aids for increasing forward movement. However, as the horse responds to these aids, rather than softening the contact to allow the additional movement, the rider's hands remain momentarily still. The seat and legs are, therefore, pushing the horse's back end forward into a gently restraining rein contact. This slight 'compression' of the horse is a basic collecting effect: as he engages a little more, his balance improves and his forehand lightens – the object has been achieved. *The moment* that the rider feels the increased engagement of the hind limbs, and the lightening of the forehand, the aids are eased – rein contact fractionally before driving aids. Unless the half-halt was made in preparation for a specific action, such as a transition, the aids revert to their state prior to the half-halt. If the hands only were

• *The half-halt, a combination of seat, leg and rein aids, is used to improve the horse's balance and heighten his attention.*

eased, the continued seat and leg aids would be asking the horse for *more* forward movement than he was showing before. If the seat and legs were eased, while the hands kept restraining, forward movement would be discouraged.

The reason why the half-halt is so named, is, in fact, that the aids represent the *first part* of asking for a full halt (if the aids were protracted a little longer, and perhaps a little more marked, the horse would step forward into halt, at which point the leg aids would be eased). This does not mean, however, that the half-halt should be seen as being halfway to halt *in terms of loss of forward movement* – i.e. the horse's speed slowing by half, or the horse nearly stopping. If anything like this happens, the aids have been applied much too strongly for far too long. Properly applied, a half-halt should last for just a moment (literally a second or less) – it is often described as taking place 'within a stride'.

It will be obvious from this description that a single half-halt is not a big action which has a big, long-lasting effect. It is a subtle action and its effect, while important and useful, may not last for long. In order to maintain quality of movement, especially in a partly schooled, unbalanced horse, it may be necessary to make half-halts quite frequently. So long as each one is ridden properly, for a genuine purpose, this is absolutely fine, and each will make a small contribution to improving the horse's balance and responsiveness.

STIFFNESS

Symptoms
1. Moving limbs stiffly and perhaps stepping short at the start of work.
2. Difficulty in rounding the spine, engaging the hind limbs.
3. Difficulty in bending correctly on turns.

Causes and cures
1. Stiffness at the start of work can result from age, wear and tear or infirmity. Depending upon the cause, it may wear off as the horse warms up. With such horses, it is quite pointless to make real demands until the stiffness has passed. If stiffness lasts more than a few minutes and/or is severe, seek veterinary advice.

The day after a hard day's work, most horses will be generally stiff in their muscles. Twenty minutes light exercise will do wonders in reducing this stiffness, but again, do not be too demanding.

2. Difficulty in rounding the spine may be a consequence of rigid skeletal conformation (examples given in Chapter 5), or may be the result of damage to the muscles or vertebrae of the back. Seek advice from a genuine, qualified equine back specialist before proceeding with training. DO NOT ATTEMPT TO USE GADGETS without consulting such an expert.

Short-term stiffness of the back and hind limbs can be the result of nervous tension (see Rhythm too Fast).

3. Difficulty in bending correctly on turns may be the result of wear and tear or specific injury, but by far the most common cause is lateral muscular stiffness. This will manifest itself in the ridden horse as crookedness and it is discussed more fully in the following section.

CROOKEDNESS

Symptoms

The horse's hind feet do not step in the same tracks as his forefeet (or keep parallel to them, if performing lateral work). Therefore, he is not consistently straight when moving on straight lines, and he does not bend correctly or with ease when turning and circling.

Causes and cures

The chief cause of crookedness is Nature – virtually all horses are naturally crooked to some extent. We will explore this phenomenon, and what to do about it, in a moment, but first let us look briefly at other contributory factors. These are:

Lack of balance. See causes and cures on page 55.

Inactivity. This does not actually cause crookedness but, if a horse (perhaps a youngster) is a little 'wandery', his natural tendency to go crooked will be reduced if he is ridden actively forward (in much the same way as you will wobble if you try

to ride a bike very slowly, but will find it easier to keep straight if you pedal more purposefully). However, it is important to differentiate between 'activity' and 'hurrying'. If you hurry a horse who is laterally stiff, he may try to make extra use of his stronger side (see below), which will increase his crookedness.

Bad riding. Especially using the outside rein as a brake, pulling the horse round a corner with the inside rein and always performing rising trot on the same diagonal. The cure is simply to avoid these errors. (In the case of the last, remembering when out hacking to change occasionally.)

Rider crookedness. We all want our horses to go straight, but very few of us are straight ourselves. Postural crookedness in the rider will have unbalancing effects upon the horse, some of which may be quite subtle. While it is fairly obvious that a rider who sits very crooked will unbalance a horse, it may also be the case that a markedly one-sided rider (for example one who is very left-handed) will unwittingly apply one leg aid more strongly than the other, or unconsciously carry one hand higher than the other, or take a stronger rein contact with that hand.

This is another reason why it is important for riders to keep checking their posture (or, preferably, have it monitored by an experienced observer). It is also valuable to remain truly aware of any such problems in oneself, especially if they are likely to mirror and compound problems in the horse. If, for example, a very left-handed rider is training a horse who finds it hard to bend to the right, both horse and rider are likely to find work on the right rein difficult. Although the rider being aware of this fact will not make the situation any *easier*, this awareness will have a value, because the sensible rider is likely to be satisfied with gradual progress and will be less inclined to try drastic, counter-productive measures.

Let us move on from these subsidiary causes of crookedness to examine natural (inherent) crookedness. Natural crookedness exists in horses in the same way that 'handedness' exists in people – in the horse, the consequence is that his whole body will be naturally curved somewhat to the left or the right. If, for example, he is curved (concave) to the left, he will turn readily to the left, but find it harder to turn to the right. Also, the fact

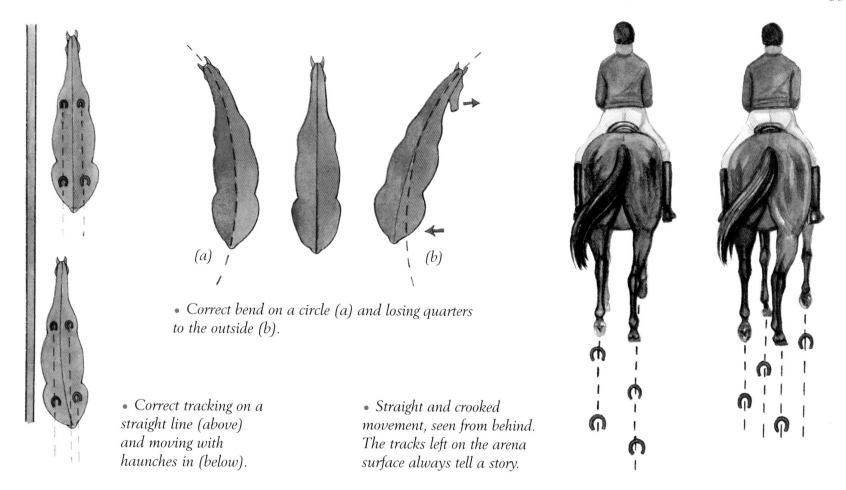

• Correct bend on a circle (a) and losing quarters to the outside (b).

• Correct tracking on a straight line (above) and moving with haunches in (below).

• Straight and crooked movement, seen from behind. The tracks left on the arena surface always tell a story.

that a horse's body is crooked will self-evidently make it difficult for him to move straight forward – in order to do something that approximates to this, he (and the rider) will have to make continual adjustments. These difficulties in moving are compounded by the effect that crookedness has on the horse's 'rear engine'. Because he is crooked, his left and right hindquarters will not be in correct (straight alignment), so they will not propel him in a truly straight line, or with completely equal force. Instead, they will tend to accentuate[3] his crookedness, which will place the quarters further out of alignment.

This natural crookedness can give rise to various biomechanical complexities, but the obvious problem that needs to be addressed is that of lateral stiffness. If a horse's body is almost permanently curved in one direction, then the lateral muscles on the inside of the curve will be relatively contracted and shortened while those on the outside will be relatively stretched. If the horse is to be made straighter, the muscles (and the associated tissues) on the inside will have to be developed so that the horse can stretch (bend) to either side with equal facility.

It will be as well here to clarify the common terminology of 'soft' and 'stiff' sides. The term 'soft' is commonly used to describe the side to which the horse bends easily (his concave side), while 'stiff' is used to describe the side to which he bends with difficulty (his convex side). This, in terms of the rider's

[3] Indeed, a natural tendency for one hind limb to be stronger than the other (dominant) may be an additional factor in crookedness.

experience, is sensible enough, and we will stay with this terminology in this book. However, it is worth remembering that these terms do not reflect *the state of the musculature* on the relevant sides of the horse. One reason why a horse will bend easily to his 'soft' side is because the muscles on the *opposite* ('stiff') side of his body will stretch readily, and one reason why he will have difficulty bending to his 'stiff' side is because the muscles on the *opposite* ('soft') side of his body are relatively tight.

Another point that requires clarification is the common misconception that crookedness is all about the horse's 'stiff' side. Because this is the side to which, for example, it may be difficult to obtain the correct canter lead, this is deemed to be the problem side. Well, it is a problem but, as we've just seen, the whole of the problem is not rooted in the side to which it is immediately obvious. Furthermore, the 'soft' side presents difficulties of its own since, on this side, the horse will be reluctant to really step forward into the rider's hand. Just as the 'stiff' side is too stiff, so the 'soft' side is too soft. The overall problem with crookedness is not that the horse is hard to bend in one direction – it is that he is crooked.

So, what is to be done about this problem? In the first place, it cannot be ignored ('Oh, his right rein has always been his bad rein'). As we have seen, the nature of crookedness is such that ignoring it must cause it to worsen and, the worse it gets, the more it will affect all aspects of the horse's work. In confronting it, however, it is important to bear in mind that:

1. Although crookedness is not a desirable state in the horse, it is (unless otherwise induced) a natural one. Therefore, remember that much of the resistance you will encounter is a consequence of physical (and perhaps mental[4]) difficulty on the horse's part, rather than sheer cussedness.

2. Although much of the remedial work must concentrate on stretching and suppling the horse's stiff muscles on his concave side, and making it easier for him to bend to his

---

[4] There is an informed view that natural crookedness in horses may be related to genetics and brain function, in much the same way as 'handedness' in humans. Therefore, the horse's difficulties may, in part, be more deep-rooted than the asymmetrical muscular development that results from them.

'stiff' side, crookedness is not a one-sided problem. Working exclusively on his 'stiff' side would be:

(a) to ignore the problems on his 'soft' (concave) side

(b) counter-productive in terms of impulsion and submission. If a horse is continually asked to do work that he finds difficult, it will be no surprise if he becomes less active and cooperative. Therefore, alternating the work from one rein to the other not only addresses the two-sided nature of crookedness, but also serves to freshen the horse up.

CIRCLE WORK

So far as specific remedies are concerned, a basic but useful exercise is circling. When circling on the horse's 'stiff' (convex) rein, the first consideration is to work on a large circle. The value of the exercise lies in him circling correctly, which he will find hard enough to do on a big circle, let alone a small one. Asking him to work on a small circle before he can perform a large one correctly will not increase the effectiveness of the exercise, it will simply mean that it will be performed incorrectly, and thus be valueless or counter-productive.

The next consideration is that the horse must be ridden actively forward. We have just noted that asking a horse to do something he finds difficult is unlikely to increase his natural impulsion, so the rider must make sure that plenty is imparted. This work is best performed in an active trot, which has more energy than walk and offers fewer complications than canter. (If a horse is *very* one-sided, cantering circles on his 'stiff' side poses enough of a problem in itself. In such circumstances it makes sense to at least partially alleviate the one-sidedness at trot *before* addressing it in canter.)

The third point is that the horse must be encouraged to take correct bend, so that he stretches the outside of his body – which is the object of the exercise. This must be achieved by a channelling effect of the rider's legs. The inside leg must act firmly on the girth, to encourage the horse to step through with his inside hind, and to provide a focal point around which the horse can flex his ribcage. The rider's outside leg, held behind the girth, provides the far bank of the channel and, importantly, holds in place the hindquarters, which will almost certainly have a tendency to swing out.

It is absolutely essential, during this exercise, that the rider does not attempt to pull the horse round the circle with the inside rein. This is always a grave error (see Circles, Chapter 10) but, in this context, especially so. In the first place, since the horse's natural bend is away from the direction of the circle, he will be quite happy to lean on the rider's inside hand. Then, if the pressure on the inside rein is sufficient, this will invite the horse to rotate his head to the inside and his quarters to the outside, so that he is going round on the wrong bend on two tracks – which will destroy the exercise and rob it of any benefit. Another possibility is that he may respond to the pressure of the inside rein by bending his neck to the inside, while keeping the rest of his body bent the other way. If this happens, the rider will have replaced a single incorrect curvature with a doubly incorrect 'S' bend!

When circling on the horse's 'soft' (concave) rein, the object is to get him to stretch forward into his inside rein. Left to his own devices on this rein, the horse will have a tendency to spiral inwards (make the circle smaller), so it can be useful to do the opposite, starting with a relatively small (say 15 m) circle and gradually and deliberately spiralling out to 20 m. Again, it is important to begin the exercise with good, active movement (which can be obtained by going large round the arena) and for the figure to be channelled primarily by the rider's legs.

When changing from circling on one rein to the other, or as respite from circling, active work on straight lines can be very helpful. This gives the horse the opportunity to engage his hips and shoulders on both sides equally, and to use the lateral muscles equally, and the extent to which he does so (the extent to which he seems straighter) will give the rider some indication of progress.

SHOULDER-IN

Another classical exercise for improving lateral suppleness (and thus alleviating crookedness) is shoulder-in. This exercise is not required in dressage tests at the lower levels. It is described here because of its value but, as with circle work, if it is not performed correctly, this value is lost. If shoulder-in is new to you, we strongly recommend that you first practise it under instruction until you are familiar with the correct feel.

Shoulder-in is a lateral exercise in which the horse is bent throughout his body around the rider's inside leg and moves forward with his body at an angle of about 30 degrees to the direction of travel. When he moves in this manner, rather than both hind feet stepping into the prints of the forefeet (as in straight work), the outside hind foot follows one track, the outside fore and *inside* hind follow pretty much the same (second) track and the inside fore follows a third track. This, at any rate, is the textbook form of the movement. Very supple and highly schooled horses may be able to perform a four-track version, moving at a greater angle, in which distinct tracks are made by outside hind, inside hind, outside fore and inside fore. More relevant to our purpose, there is also a lesser form of the exercise, known as shoulder-fore, in which the horse's inside hind forms a track between the tracks of the forefeet, and the horse's body moves at a significantly reduced angle.

Devised centuries ago, shoulder-in has many benefits, which include promoting freedom of the shoulders and producing a collecting effect. In the context of crookedness, it chief values are to encourage engagement of the inside hind leg, and to stretch the outside lateral muscles. It also makes the horse step into the outside rein. Therefore, when it is ridden on the horse's 'stiff' side, it is acting on key parts in the following ways:

1. Encouraging the hind leg on the 'stiff' (convex) side to step forward and engage underneath the body.
2. Promoting a stretching of the tight lateral muscles of the horse's concave side (now on the outside).
3. Encouraging the horse to reach into the outside rein and take a proper contact on what is normally his 'soft' side.

If these benefits are to be achieved, it will be necessary to introduce the exercise with some thought and care. Setting up major resistances or evasions, or performing a travesty of the movement, will be pointless. Therefore, you should give consideration to the following:

1. Shoulder-in is a lateral movement, so introducing it presupposes that the horse already understands the idea of moving sideways away from your leg. The two exercises usually used

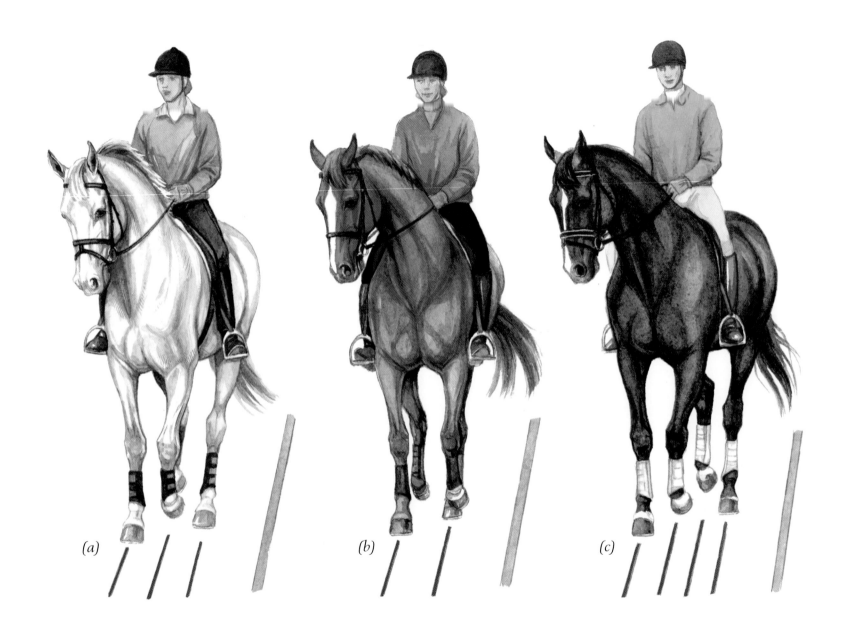

(a)   (b)   (c)

• *Forms of shoulder-in.*
(a) Correct three-track version.
(b) Incorrect: the horse is simply moving along the wall with his neck bent to the inside.

(c) Four-track version. This can be performed correctly by very supple horses, who can bend their bodies and flex their joints substantially. However, if the horse moves at an angle on four tracks, but with virtually no bend, he is more or less leg-yielding down the wall.

to teach this are turns on the forehand and leg-yielding. If the horse is *not yet obedient* to lateral leg aids, he must learn them first. Trying to teach this *at the same time* as teaching shoulder-in would be asking too much.

2. In all lateral work, it is an inviolate rule that forward movement takes precedence over sideways movement. The horse is asked for active forward movement, then some of the existing energy is converted into sideways movement. Therefore, the horse must be able to show consistent activity when going straight forward before he can be asked to go sideways.

• *Shoulder-in, showing the inside hind leg stepping forward and under the horse's body.*

3. Shoulder-in can be ridden in walk, trot and (technically) canter[5], but its main gymnastic benefits will be gained in trot. At walk, the horse does not generate enough energy to produce much of a suppling effect. However, it can be helpful to introduce the *idea* of the movement at walk, especially if the rider is also new to it, or the horse is a little slow on the uptake.

4. Although you will want to concentrate a significant amount of this work on the horse's 'stiff' side, it will be harder for him to do it in this direction. Therefore, when first introducing the exercise, it makes sense to ride it on the horse's 'soft' side. Since he must first learn what to do, he is more likely to listen and cooperate if you ask him to do something he finds reasonably easy.

5. Further to this, remember that the first object of teaching a horse something new is to get the penny to drop. The horse showing some recognition of what is required, and some willingness to comply, is a major step. The greater the angle you ask for initially, the harder it will be for the horse to respond *correctly* (even on his 'soft' side). Therefore, proceed slowly – ensure a correct response at a lesser angle (more like shoulder-fore) before asking for more.

6. Remember that the exercise is only of value while it is being performed correctly, and it is only of value in the learning stage if the horse is working along the right lines and is not seeking actively to evade. Three correct steps are vastly more useful than thirteen incorrect or deteriorating ones. Therefore, be satisfied with just a little correct work and always ride the horse actively straight forward out of the movement ideally before, but certainly the moment, that the quality becomes lost. Similarly, if an attempt patently goes wrong from the start, do not struggle to retrieve the irretrievable, but re-establish the gait on a straight line and try again.

[5] A slight *shoulder-fore* position may help produce a better strike-off into canter from a horse who has difficulties with a particular lead. However, attempting full-blown shoulder-in at canter on a horse who is not already properly balanced and supple would be a recipe for disaster. The suppling work is done in trot.

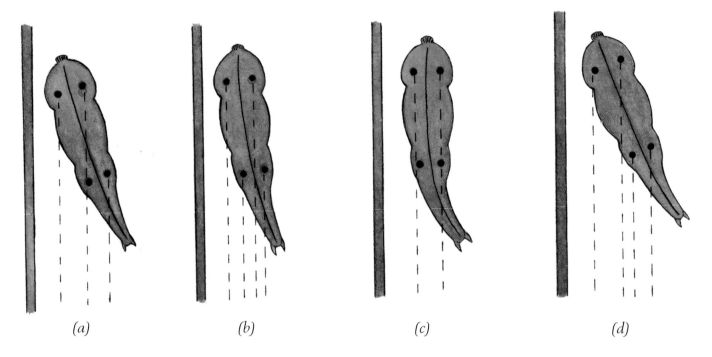

(a)   (b)   (c)   (d)*

Shoulder-in is most frequently ridden along the wall of the arena and this is certainly the easiest place to begin, since the wall will help prevent the horse from evading the exercise by swinging his quarters out and will create a definitive line for horse and rider. A common recommendation is to precede the shoulder-in by starting a 10 m circle on the centre line then begin to ask for shoulder-in as you touch the long side, the idea being that this will create the desired bend. While this will set up a reasonably well-schooled and supple horse for the thirty-degree shoulder-in, it may be rather too demanding for less well-schooled horses in the early stages, the main reason being that, if the horse cannot perform an accurate, active 10 m circle, the setting-up value will be lost. Therefore, it may be more useful to begin with a somewhat larger figure, of such size that activity and accuracy are maintained. (If these qualities still become lost, don't start the exercise until they are restored.). It is also possible to start the circle from the long side (say a 15 m circle from E, beginning the shoulder-in on return to E, at the start of a second circle) since, in the early stages, only very few steps will be required. The essence of riding the movement is as follows.

- *Diagrams of shoulder-in.*
(a) Correct, three-track movement at an angle of 30 degrees, with lateral bend.
(b) Correct shoulder-fore.
(c) Incorrect: bend in neck only.
(d) A form sometimes called 'three-and-a-half track': this is sometimes produced unintentionally simply by asking for too great an angle, which may compromise the 'forward' element.

As the horse starts the first stride of a new circle which would take him away from the long side of the arena, the rider sit up extra straight (braces the back) and closes the fingers of the outside hand, thus producing a mild half-halt. The rider's inside leg applies pressure, asking the horse to step forwards and sideways along the outside track (arena wall). The inside leg is the main motivating aid, encouraging the horse to maintain the bend and engage his inside hind. In applying this aid, the rider must be careful not to lean over and collapse the inside hip in an over-enthusiastic attempt to drive the horse sideways. The rider's outside leg, which is slightly behind the girth (where it would have been positioned for the circle) is ready to prevent any attempt by the horse to swing his quarters out (the wall will also help in this respect, but in some arenas it is not possible to ride close enough to the wall for it to be a physical barrier[6]). By maintaining a passive but definite contact (resting but not driving) with the horse's side, this leg also helps to channel the energy generated by the rider's inside leg, so that the horse is encouraged to work forward into his bridle and sideways, rather than just running or falling sideways.

Human beings have an entirely natural tendency to use their hands for steering and controlling, and shoulder-in is one movement where there is a temptation to do too much in this respect. While the horse is moving in shoulder-in, the main function of the rider's outside hand is to prevent any tendency for the horse to bend his neck too much to the inside (which he may well try to do, especially on his 'soft' side). This does not mean that rider should automatically hang on to this rein (if the horse bends correctly and works into this rein, there will be a slight increase in contact anyway), but that the hand should remain receptive to any warning signal coming from the horse. The main function of the inside hand, once it has helped to guide the horse into the appropriate degree of bend, is to remain as quiet as possible. As when circling, attempting to bend the whole horse with the inside rein will simply cause too much bend in the neck and provoke the hindquarters into escaping to the outside.

Learning to coordinate the aids, especially on a horse who is not particularly compliant, may take some time. Briefly, indications of common errors are as follows:

Loss of impulsion/activity. Too much emphasis on going sideways, at the expense of forward movement.

Too much bend in the horse's neck and not enough in his body, coupled with lack of engagement of his inside hind leg. Overuse of inside rein and ineffective use of legs (especially inside leg) to frame or position the horse.

A more or less straight angle in the horse's body, rather than bend. The horse is verging on leg-yielding, which is a different exercise, lacking the gymnastic benefits of shoulder-in. This may indicate incorrect set-up, the horse being driven sideways by the rider's inside leg with no framing back-up from the outside leg; outside rein contact too strong or even being used to pull the horse up the track.

If such mistakes can be avoided or eradicated, shoulder-in can bring great benefits to training. Furthermore, familiarity with this work will assist both horse and rider as they progress, in time, to other forms of lateral work.

Before leaving this subject of crookedness, we should mention a subtle form that can occur if the horse gets into the habit of keeping both his outside shoulder and hip parallel to the wall of the school ('leaning on the wall'). Because a horse is narrower at the shoulders than the hips, this has the effect of him going 'quarters in'. The effect may be greater when he is going round the arena on his 'stiff' rein, because he will naturally tend to be bent towards his soft side, which will be the outside. This can make certain movements, such as transitions to correct canter lead, especially difficult.

This form of crookedness can cause problems even for advanced riders on well-schooled horses, and it is not the first problem you would tackle on a partly trained one. However, you can at least avoid encouraging it by being sure to sit straight yourself, and not hanging on to the outside rein. Active forward riding on straight lines away from the wall (Chapter 10) and counter-canter (Chapter 9) also play their part in correcting such crookedness.

HOLLOW OUTLINE (ABOVE THE BIT)

Symptoms

The horse carries his head artificially high and does not take a proper contact with the bit. There may be a lot of muscular development underneath his neck. The 'hollow' topline will make it difficult for the horse to engage his hind legs properly – if he is frightened of going forwards into the rider's hands, he will not *want* to engage his hind limbs.

[6] And, at a later stage, the movement may not be ridden along the wall.

Causes and cures

1. Conformation flaws. See Chapter 5 for suggestions as to how to work with these.
2. Injury to mouth, tooth trouble, pain from badly fitting tack. Remedy before continuing schooling.
3. The most common cause of this problem is bad riding; the rider sitting 'behind the movement' and hanging on to the reins. For information on correct posture and aid applications, see Chapter 2.

If you take on a horse who has been 'ridden hollow' over a long period, and he does have a lot of muscle underneath his neck, you will not be able to cure the problem overnight. It may take some time to get him confident to accept a contact and, even when he is *willing* to lower his head and neck, it will not be easy for him to do so while there is a great mass of muscle holding his neck up like a surgical collar.

If, at first, he is frightened of taking a contact, you will have to ride him quietly in walk and trot on a virtually loose rein. Do this in an enclosed space because, if he takes fright and tries to run off in a situation where you *have* to stop him quickly, doing so will only aggravate the problem. When trotting, sit lightly and rise quietly. Try, so far as possible, to slow down and stop by using your seat and back, with absolutely minimal rein aids. Give the horse time to learn that it is all right to lower his head before you start making any demands of him.

Once the horse shows signs that he is losing his fear of the hands, you can start asking him to listen to them. Work in trot, making simple, frequent changes of direction. Have the reins at a more normal length, and take a definite, but *light*, contact. If the horse has markedly 'soft' and 'stiff sides', start by keeping your contact on the 'soft' (concave) side still, because the horse is more likely to accept a contact on that side. With your other hand, periodically ask the horse to flex his jaw a little by making a *gentle* squeezing action with your fingers. Close the fingers gradually, then open them gradually, as if you were giving a young child's hand a reassuring squeeze. The more subtle you can make this action, the better response you will get. THE ACTION MUST BE OF THE FINGERS ONLY – DO NOT PULL BACK WITH THE HAND.

If the horse shows any resistance, continue the squeezing contact and send him more forward with your leg on the same side. The moment his resistance ceases, ease the leg aid and soften the rein contact. If, instead of resisting, he responds by relaxing and lowering his head and neck even a little, praise him and ease your hands to encourage him to stretch forwards and down.

At first, do this work for short periods only. Between times, let the horse walk on a long rein. Gradually, he will learn to accept the rein contact, and his outline will become less hollow. Be patient; remember that you are trying to *help* the horse to move in a way that is easier and more comfortable for him. Remember, also, that he will not be able to do this on a regular basis until the necessary changes to the musculature of his neck have taken place.

HORSE BEHIND THE BIT

Symptoms

The horse carries the head and neck too low, or else 'scrunched in' in an exaggerated arch, overbending throughout the whole of the neck; his head may be well behind the vertical. He may 'run along on his shoulders', with hind legs trailing or taking short, hoppy steps. These characteristics are entirely different from those of the correctly schooled horse, who stretches his head and neck down when permitted, chewing or seeking the bit, but maintaining balance and forward movement.

- *Curing hollowness that has arisen from past bad riding can be a lengthy process. (a) The condition is produced by a rider hanging on with the hands.*
(b) Riding quietly forward on a virtually loose rein.
(c) Transitions given quietly with the seat.
(d) Beginning to ask the horse to accept a light contact.
(e) When the horse shows residual signs of resistance, the rider asks him diplomatically to step forward into a 'friendly' rein contact.
(f) Whenever the horse shows signs of accepting the contact, the rider softens it a little and praises the horse.

(a) (b) (c)

(d) (e) (f)

Causes and cures

1. The usual root cause is that a rider has, in some way, tried to impose an outline on the horse. The reason why this is wrong has been discussed in the section on Outline. The chapter on Conformation also warned against demanding too much flexion from a horse who would find it difficult. If you take on a horse who moves in this way, the precise cure will depend partly on the extent and root cause of the problem. Trying to impose an outline on the horse can be considered in two broad categories:
(a) Incorrect, rather than harsh, training. The horse's head has been 'fiddled' down too much without regard for forward movement. The horse is not actually frightened of, or trying to evade, the bit; he thinks he is doing what is required. He needs to be allowed to rediscover his natural movement. Ride him actively forward at all gaits, with a very light contact and quiet hands. Whenever he wants to stretch his neck *forwards* this must be encouraged but, if he tries to lean on the bit, or drop his head too deep into his chest, you must ride him more forward and reduce the rein contact, so that he has nothing to lean on or drop behind. Do not, on any account, try to pull, or hold, his head up.
(b) Training that has caused fear/mistrust. The horse has been forced into a false outline by harsh hands and/or a harsh bit, possibly reinforced by misused gadgets. He is very restricted in his movement and actually frightened of going forward into a rein contact. It may be necessary to start off by fitting a very mild bit (straight bar rubber or nylon snaffle) and walking on a virtually loose rein until the horse begins to show signs of stretching forwards. As progress is made, it may be possible to encourage the horse to go more forward into a contact by using situations in which his enthusiasm overcomes his fear. An example would be cantering uphill following other horses, encouraging the horse forwards on a light contact. (Choose good ground, fit boots and sit securely, because his movement and balance may not be at their best.) As the horse begins to show improvement, proceed as (a) above.

2. Evasion. Although horses usually evade the bit from fear and mistrust, there are some who learn to do so as an act of defiance; when asked to go forward into a contact, they respond by dropping behind the bit. This is often linked to a reluctance to obey the leg aids: the horse defies the rider by ignoring the leg and evading the hand. This is a very serious problem, and it has to be stressed that most horses who behave like this were, at least at some stage, provoked into it by a rider. Certainly, if this is not the case, and they are confirmed in such behaviour by their own character, then it is unlikely that they will ever be pleasant or reliable rides.

This problem is much better prevented than cured but, if it is to be cured, it will require a rider who is absolutely determined to succeed; lack of resolve and inconsistency will only serve to reinforce the horse's superiority.

Because the basic disobedience is to the leg, you must ride such a horse purposefully forward, using artificial aids if necessary to reinforce the leg. Your hands must allow the horse to respond, not only in the context of what you are trying to achieve, but also because driving such a horse into a hard rein contact might provoke a rear. You must demand more forward movement *every time* you sense it is at all lacking, and you must not be satisfied with anything less than an immediate response: the horse must become convinced that he cannot ignore your leg. Only when the horse is consistently obedient to your leg can you begin to ask him to go forward into a contact. To make him accept both leg and hand, ride lots of simple transitions. With the upward transitions, continue to expect an immediate response to the leg; lighten your hands to allow the horse forward. With downward transitions, be very careful with the rein aids. If you get any feeling that the horse is 'coming back' to the slower gait, abandon the transition and ride him forward. The correct feeling is that he continues to go forward, but changes gait. This is always the correct feeling for downward transitions, but it is *essential* in these circumstances.

- *Overbending. (a) Horse clearly behind the bit – contrast with (b) correctly trained horse stretching for the bit. (c) A common consequence of 'fiddling' the horse's head down, without regard for overall movement. (d) Beginning to cure the problem: riding actively forward with a very light contact – contrast with (e) trying to pull the horse's head up with the reins. (f) Destructive abuse of draw reins.*

(a)

(b)

(c)

(d)

(e)

(f)

(a)   *(b)*

• *Curing a horse who has become habitually overbent may take time and patience. (a) Still overbent out of habit; (b) beginning to take a contact, but not yet really stepping into it.*

ABNORMAL RESPONSES TO AIDS

We could argue that, to some extent, any horse with training flaws will respond to some aids in ways which are not normal or correct. While this is basically true, the following passage is chiefly concerned with horses in whom this is the most prevalent problem.

In the section on Anticipation in Chapter 4, we noted that a horse can learn to respond to signals which are not correct aids. He does this by association of ideas: 'The rider always tightens the reins before we canter, so tightening the reins must be a signal to canter'.

It is important to understand that such signals are not incorrect just because they offend against a view of what is correct, but because they are of limited value. Normally, they will only work to a certain extent, and they may also impair the horse's ability to interpret other aids clearly. Taking the example mentioned, it will be seen that there is little logic in teaching a horse that an increase in rein contact is the signal for an *upward* transition to canter when a brief increase in rein contact is, in other circumstances, part of the signal for a *downward* transition. Similarly, although it may be possible to persuade a horse to stop simply by pulling on the reins, the resultant halt will probably be so crooked and unbalanced that he will not be able to follow it by anything more than a mockery of a rein-back or turn on the forehand nor, indeed, will he be able to move straight and smoothly forward when required.

If you take on a horse who has learnt, by association, to respond to incorrect aids, you must remember that it is not the horse who is at fault; it is his past training. He is behaving in the way which he believes is required of him, so there is no point in blaming him for not responding correctly to your own 'textbook' aids, or for responding in a way you did not expect. Instead, you must re-educate him.

The first step along this path is to try to analyse what aids the horse responds to, and why. This may require some experimental riding on your part; you are trying to discover the language the horse understands. It may be, for example, that he will only go from walk to trot in response to quite a dig from both your heels

(a) *(b)* *(c)*

- *Horses can learn to respond to abnormal aids, but these do not benefit training. (a) The horse can be stopped by means of the reins alone, but the resultant halt will be of poor quality. (b) A strong aid with the outside leg alone may induce the horse to leap into a crooked canter, but the transition will become better and straighter as the horse learns to respond to a correct combination of aids (c).*

some way behind the girth, or that his idea of a canter aid is a great kick from your outside heel. At first, if you want him to trot or canter, these are the aids you will have to give, because they are all he understands. However, as soon as you have discovered what he believes to be the signal to do something, you can begin to re-educate him. In the first example, you can ride lots of walk to trot transitions, very gradually reducing the amount of movement and pressure of your legs until the horse

learns to respond to a little squeeze from legs which remain almost in place. In the second example, you can ride lots of transitions to canter, gradually introducing forward driving aids from your inside leg and seatbone at the same time as you reduce the amount of movement and severity of your outside leg aid. The essence of these, and all other examples of re-schooling, is that the rider starts off by 'talking' to the horse on the horse's terms, and makes changes gradually – a process similar to introducing one idea at a time when teaching something new.

In addition to improving the horse, the process of re-schooling increases the rider's understanding of equitation, and ability to 'get through' to different horses. Therefore, although there may be times when you wish it were unnecessary, you should not shrink from re-schooling, nor should you dismiss as useless any horse in need of it.

·7·

THE BASIC GAITS

The basic gaits, at which virtually all foundation work will be carried out, are known as medium[1] walk and working trot and canter. It is important to understand that these descriptions refer to something other than just walk, trot and canter. Many horses are capable of moving quite poorly in these gaits, but doing so will not advance training, nor will it satisfy a dressage judge. On the other hand, when the basic gaits are performed well, they have a value that goes beyond merely being forms of movement – they can actually contribute towards training.

Walk offers both horse and rider time to think and is therefore a useful gait in which to introduce *the idea* of new movements. It can also have a calming effect if horse, rider or both become tense. If some work has gone wrong, or if communication between horse and rider has broken down, a period of reflection at walk is much more likely to prove constructive than a bull-headed 'do it at all costs' approach. Walk also offers physical respite from the more energetic work at trot and canter. However, in this context 'rest' should be viewed as the lesser energy naturally expended in an *active* walk. The horse should not be allowed to slop around, and must not learn that walking = dossing. (The movement of free walk on a long rein is discussed in Chapter 9.)

Trot is the gait most suited to general schooling, being more impulsive than walk and less physically demanding and complex than canter. In a correct working trot, all four legs perform an equal amount of work (helping to establish balance and rhythm) and the back muscles flex and extend alternately on either side of the spine, producing a suppling effect upon the whole body.

Canter, although the most complex gait, is a very useful vehicle for improving impulsion and, performed correctly, it plays an important role in the longitudinal suppling (rounding) of the horse's back.

The working gaits are (or should be) developed in the early stages of training a young horse – by increasing the horse's strength, improving his balance and introducing a little more activity, his natural gaits are enhanced to a degree that enables him to work in rhythm and balance whilst carrying a rider. Although, in this book, we are not discussing early training in detail, you should be aware that, if you take on a young, undeveloped horse (or one who is in poor condition), it will be necessary to carry out this preliminary work to establish (or re-establish) the working gaits before any further progress can be made. This, like so much in riding, is achieved on a basis of steady progression. Through short, regular amounts of work, the horse's strength improves; as a consequence, his balance and weight-carrying capacity improve, and then he can be asked for more activity.

---

[1] In walk, the term 'medium' rather than 'working' is used. Basically, this relates to the view that, since there is no moment of suspension in walk, the horse cannot work in walk in the same way as he can in trot and canter. For practical purposes, medium walk can be considered to be the walk equivalent of working trot and canter.

So how can we tell whether the working gaits are established? In brief, the following criteria should be evident. When in motion, the horse should remain pretty evenly balanced over all four feet – he should not sag beneath the rider or be falling onto the forehand. He should show a degree of engagement of the hind limbs and should move actively forward in a consistent rhythm. He should be able and willing to remain on the aids (between leg and hand). His length of stride should be the norm for that horse[2] when he is reasonably active but not being asked for any specific adjustment or extra effort. In other words, he should be workmanlike. In a few of the Novice level dressage tests there is a limited requirement for lengthened gaits, and we will look at these in Chapter 9. For the time being, however, let us look at the individual gaits in more detail.

MEDIUM WALK

The essence of all correct movement at walk is that it should be in a regular 1.2.3.4 rhythm. In medium walk, the horse should move in this rhythm with his hind feet touching the ground a little in front of the prints made by his forefeet (over-tracking slightly). A horse of reasonable conformation, sound and healthy, *should* do this naturally if he is not interfered with. It is, in fact, much easier to spoil a good walk than to improve it so, if your horse is naturally a good walker, leave well alone! If, for example, you hack out in company and keep getting ahead of your companions because your horse walks out well, either stop occasionally, or let them trot to catch up. So long as the horse is not hurrying (out of correct rhythm), do not attempt to slow the walk down because the chances are that you will only interfere with it, producing crabby, stilted movement. This is *not* collected walk which, along with extended walk, is a very advanced movement that can be quite difficult to achieve properly.

If your horse's walk is not very good, you will have to make efforts to improve it. Aside from problems caused by faulty conformation, poor walk usually relates to either inactivity or too fast a rhythm, to which may be added poor cadence. These matters have been discussed in the previous chapter and if they are also evident in trot and canter, it is best to make significant progress in improving these gaits before concentrating on the walk.

If an inactive walk has been caused by restrictive riding, the first step towards improving it is to ride the horse on a long rein and a very light contact, allowing him full freedom of his head and neck. Walking down hills will help improve activity and length of stride, but you must choose a suitable, sound surface (not a worn out metalled road) and *allow* the horse to walk out, rather than trying to *make* him do so.

As suggested above, an idle walk is best improved by dealing with the idleness through work in other gaits, especially trot. However, if, as sometimes happens, the walk is only a little inactive and the other gaits are not, it may be that the horse will offer more activity if it is requested through firmer aids. Sitting deep but still, with a slightly braced back and applying *light* leg pressure in rhythm[3] with the walk may have the desired effect. It may be helpful to back up these leg aids with light reminder aids from the whip at any moment when an incipient loss of energy is detected. Do not, however, 'row' the horse along with your seat and upper body, because this will just unbalance him and interfere with the gait. Neither as we have seen, should you nag him incessantly with ill-timed leg aids that go on and off his sides in pairs.

When a horse hurries in walk, his movement becomes more of a 1.2, 1.2 rhythm because the legs on each side tend towards stepping as pairs rather than each leg stepping in a separate,

[2] It is a general rule of thumb that, in the working gaits, a horse should track up (his hind feet should step pretty much into the prints made by the corresponding forefeet) and in medium walk he should over-track slightly (the hind feet step slightly beyond the prints of the forefeet). In the vast majority of cases, such stepping is a fairly accurate indicator of appropriate movement and, for practical purposes (and throughout this chapter) it can be considered the norm. However, a horse's tracking is not the only criterion by which his gaits can be assessed. The relative length of his body, various other physical proportions and the angulation and action of his limbs all contribute to the manner in which he moves. Therefore, if you have a horse of unusual conformation you should not become hidebound in assessing his gaits *solely* on the basis of his tracking. For example, a very long-bodied horse might be showing a good, active trot ('working' in every other sense) and yet be under-tracking a little (hind feet stepping just short of the prints of the forefeet). Overall quality and feel of the gait are important elements in assessing it.
[3] This means that the legs are applied one at a time as the horse steps forward with the corresponding hind leg. This movement should be felt quite readily through the seat, the other clue being that, as the hind leg steps forward, there will be a slight but definite bulging of the ribcage on the same side. In fact, if the rider's leg is resting correctly against the horse's side, this slight bulging into the leg will pretty much result in the horse giving himself a light aid, which the rider can accentuate if necessary. (Novice riders who are unable, initially, to interpret these sensations can ask a friend to call out as the horse moves the relevant leg – 'left hind, right hind…')

distinct way. We have previously discussed reasons why a horse may hurry and, if the fault occurs because you are being too 'busy', the answer is to sit more quietly. You should also consider this if it is the horse who is too 'busy', whether through temperament or circumstance. As mentioned, steadying the walk without constricting it is by no means easy, but if you are sure that a hurried rhythm is coming solely from the horse and is not a result of incorrect aids, you can help steady it by keeping a consistent (but not heavy) rein contact, sitting still and deep, and keeping your legs resting quietly against the horse's sides. It may help if you think positively of being still, like a mounted statue. Circle work and riding walk in shoulder-fore (see previous chapter) may help, as may walking up steep hills.

Work over ground poles can also help to regulate a poor walk, whether inactive or hurried. It is preferable for the poles to have blocks of some sort at each end so that they cannot be easily dislodged. (Cavalletti have rather gone out of favour in recent times but, if they are used, they should be set on their lowest height.)

There should be four poles, to allow for a full stride of walk. They are best located down a long side of the arena, just in from the outside track. Their spacing is crucial to what you are trying to achieve so, in the first place, they must be spaced evenly. Second, their spacing may have to be adjusted to achieve the aim, which is for the horse to walk through them in an even 1.2.3.4 rhythm with slight over-tracking. A knowledgeable assistant on the ground is almost essential to help with this.

The precise spacing you will require will depend upon the individual horse, and it may be necessary to adjust it if you have to achieve your aim little by little. As a rough guide, with an average-sized horse, you can use a distance between poles of about 0.9 m (3 ft) as a starting point, tending towards a slightly long distance if you are trying to make the horse more active and a slightly short one if you are trying to prevent him from hurrying.

• *Correct sequence of legs in walk (above) and the walk tending towards two-time (below).*

• *Using ground poles to improve the walk. In this case, the poles are being used to encourage free, active steps and a stretching of the topline. The rider's leg is a little far forward.*

Before you ride over the line of poles, walk the horse a couple of times over a single pole, to engage his attention. When you approach the line of poles, ensure that the horse is straight. Keep him moving forwards and keep your hands light. Do not try to place him at the poles – let the poles regulate his steps. If he wants to stretch his neck down to look at the poles or assist his balance, allow him to do so, but not at the expense of losing forward movement (leg aids keep him active). Depending upon how the horse moves through the poles, ask your assistant to adjust them until the required walk is achieved.

However, achieving the desired walk through the poles is really the starting point. Do not think of them as the one place where you can obtain a good walk. Instead, think of them as an aid to obtaining the first steps, feel the rhythm and try to maintain it as you ride round the school. If, at first, you cannot maintain it for long, do not go right round the arena losing the walk, but ride a smaller figure so that you go through the poles more frequently or, alternatively, set up a second line of poles opposite the first.

WORKING TROT

In working trot, the rhythm should be a businesslike but unhurried 1.2., 1.2. The horse should move actively forwards in a balanced manner and his hind feet should step pretty much into the prints of his forefeet (tracking up).

Because the gait is two-time, with the legs moving in diagonal pairs, trot is the most mechanically simple of the gaits, and the one in which the horse can most easily find and keep rhythm and balance. Also, the action of the horse's feet striking the ground at trot produces more kinetic energy than is the case at walk, and thus assists in maintaining impulsion.

With all these advantages, we can see that a horse should be able to perform a reasonable working trot quite readily and, indeed, the gait is easier to improve, and harder to spoil, than walk. If the trot is poor, this is usually the result of one of the training flaws which, together with their remedies, were discussed earlier.

As with walk, pole work can be used to help improve and regulate the trot. The same general principles are applied, but the spacing of the poles must be altered to take account of the different stride pattern. As a rough guide, use a spacing of 1.3 – 1.4 m (4 ft 3 in – 4 ft 7 in) as a starting point for the average horse. When trotting over poles, it can sometimes be useful to set them at a greater height than for walk, to encourage a horse to round his back and pick his feet up. You should not, however, overdo this, or use it in an attempt at *forcing* improvement from a horse who hurries to any great extent, or who is markedly hollow-backed/ewe-necked, because it will probably just confuse or frighten him, or even cause a stumble or fall. Instead, with such horses, you should look for gradual improvement, first on the flat and then through a set up which will not punish errors or carelessness too severely.

SITTING AND RISING TROT

While we are discussing trot, it might be useful to look briefly at the alternatives of sitting and rising. Basically, sitting trot places the rider in a position of full control, and it should be used whenever such control is needed. However, its benefit (to horse and rider) depends upon the rider having attained a good basic posture, and a consequent ability of the muscles of the seat to act as a shock absorber (see Chapter 2). If the rider's upper body and hands are unsteady, this will inevitably have a negative

- *Sequence of legs at trot.*

• *Using slightly raised poles to regulate the trot.*

• *Incorrect use of trotting poles – they are set too high, worrying the horse and causing him to rush.*

influence on the quality of the trot, however good it would otherwise be. Furthermore, a rider who is desperately attempting to sit rigidly in the saddle, without the seat absorbing the horse's motion, will simply pound up and down on the horse's back and drive him into a hollow outline. This is yet more evidence of the need to establish correct posture, as discussed earlier.

Although the rider's contact with the horse is somewhat diminished in rising trot, this form (performed correctly) is easier on the horse's back than sitting trot. It is used (except in moments of emergency) as standard practice on a young horse and it is similarly useful on older horses who have under-developed or otherwise weak backs, and on horses who have become hollow-backed through bad riding.

The essence of rising to the trot is that the rider simply eases the buttocks slightly off the saddle, taking more weight on the thighs. There should be no daylight beneath the rider's seat, which should not be prized out of the saddle by overt actions of the knees or ankles. Rising too high will simply disconnect the rider's seat from communication with the horse and will compromise the use of the rider's legs. Furthermore, it will almost certainly result in the rider coming down 'behind' the horse's movement. This sort of rising – which may also be associated with using the reins for balance – has no beneficial effect whatsoever.

Much lip service is paid to the need, especially when hacking, to change the diagonal upon which one is rising at regular intervals. In practice, many riders don't do this, but rise habitually on the comfortable diagonal – the one favoured by the horse. This omission merely overloads one diagonal and will contribute further to the existing stiffness and crookedness.

So far as dressage tests are concerned, it is currently permissible, under British Dressage rules, to perform trot work in Preliminary and Novice Level tests either sitting or rising. In more advanced tests, unless otherwise specified on the test sheet, all trot work must be performed sitting. This ruling may not necessarily apply to tests ridden under the rules of other organising bodies, so it is always sensible to check this point at the time of entering the competition.

• *Elements of incorrect rising trot. Here, the rider's stirrup leathers are slightly too long so, during the sitting phase, she is reaching for the stirrups and her upper body has tilted just behind the vertical. As she rises, she stretches her legs further in an attempt to retain her stirrups, rising from her stirrups rather than from her thighs. In consequence, she rises too far out of the saddle, and her upper body tips further backwards. She is now on the verge of having to retain some semblance of balance by supporting herself on the reins. When this happens, her hands and upper body position will be stifling the horse's forward movement, and her seat and legs will not be in the right position to ask the horse for more. Therefore, the trot will became less and less active.*

WORKING CANTER

Working canter should have a regular, active but unhurried 1.2.3., 1.2.3 rhythm, with the horse tracking up. The sequence of footfall at canter (one hind leg, the opposite hind leg together with its diagonal foreleg, then the 'leading' foreleg) makes it harder for the horse to maintain balance and straightness than in walk or trot. Although conformation and natural balance play important parts, the quality of a horse's canter will also be affected by the extent to which he was suppled, strengthened and balanced before he was first asked to canter.

Because their underlying influences are so great, any relevant flaws in conformation or training must be taken into account when dealing with problems in canter. In brief, the major problems and their likely underlying causes are:

Wrong lead. An isolated wrong lead may simply be caused by poor application of the aids, or a moment's inattention by the horse. Persistent wrong lead (a marked reluctance to canter on one rein) usually relates to marked one-sided stiffness/crookedness. In such cases, the best course of action is to remedy the underlying problem (taking such time as is necessary) through exercises in trot before returning to canter, by which point the difficulty should be significantly reduced.

If a horse who has previously been willing to canter on both leads suddenly develops an aversion to one particular lead, it is almost certain that this relates to some undiagnosed physical problem. In such a case, do not assume that the horse is being difficult – consult your vet.

A relative difficulty in cantering on one rein. Horse canters reasonably well on one lead, but sometimes fails to take/sustain the correct lead on the other rein; feels unbalanced; readily breaks into trot, especially on circles. These symptoms suggest a lesser degree of the stiffness/crookedness displayed by the horse who persistently takes a wrong lead – they might even be signs of relative improvement in such a horse. Again, further suppling and straightening work in trot is indicated. Also, before asking for the transition into canter, it can be useful to set the horse up in shoulder-fore, as this positioning will assist him to take the correct lead. However, do not overdo this, or become too reliant on it, as it may become difficult to get the horse to canter straight.

• *(Facing page) Sequence of legs in (right) canter.*

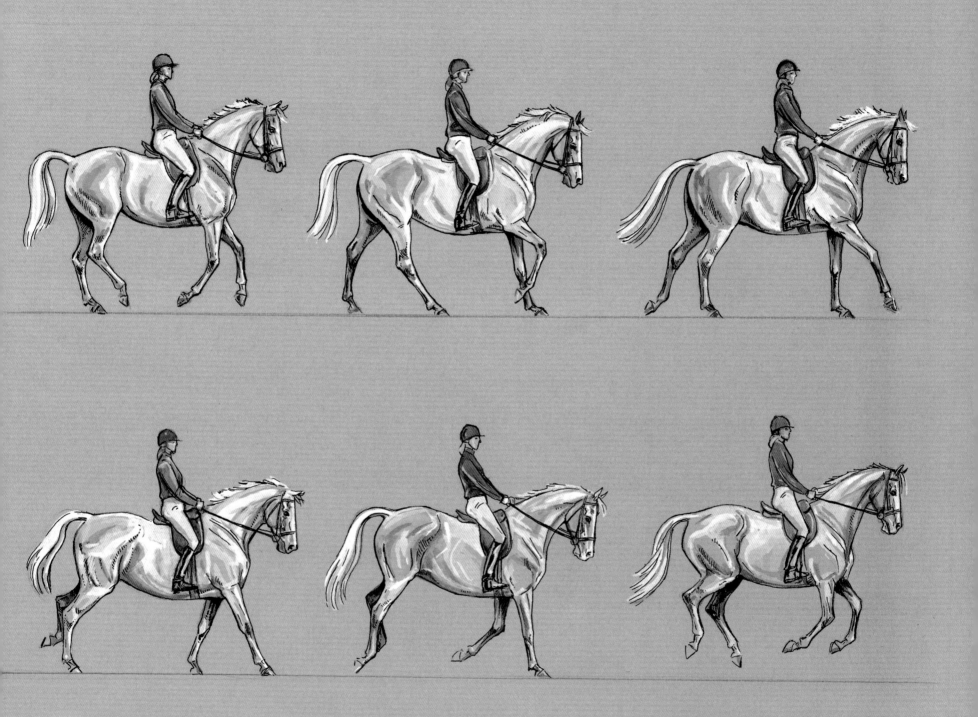

● *Disunited canter. Compare with sequence of correct movement on page 79.*

Cantering disunited. This is an odd form of movement, in which the horse still moves in pretty much in three-time, but with an incorrect sequence of footfall (left leg 'leading' in front and right leg 'leading' behind, or vice versa). It is sometimes seen in more advanced horses who have performed 'half' of a flying change, but may also be evidence of one-sidedness, lack of balance and weakness, especially in young or inexperienced horses who have been asked to canter too soon. Once more, in such cases, attending to the underlying problems is the key to progress. However, it is also worth noting that some horses will change behind as a form of evasion if the rider is restricting their forward movement. If this appears to the case, the rider should check the overall rein contact and ensure especially that the outside rein is not too restrictive. If this form of evasion seems to relate to the horse being simply over-excited, it may be useful to do some calming work in walk and trot, slipping quietly back into canter once he has settled down.

Disconnected movement. This covers oddities such as trotting behind and cantering in front, and is often rooted in conformation defects, for example a combination of heavy shoulders and poor hindquarters, or a long back coupled with trailing hocks and a high (up and down) action of the limbs. It may be exacerbated by a rider trying to 'chase' the horse into canter from a running trot, rather than establishing adequate balance and activity and then attempting the transition[4]. Where conformation flaws contribute to this problem, doing whatever is practical to minimise their effect can only help (for example, building up the muscle on inadequate hindquarters). Cantering uphill, in a straight line on good ground, may help to regulate the gait, and early attempts at turning and circling should be avoided.

Unlike walk and trot, canter work over poles or cavalletti as an aid to improving a poor canter has little to recommend it, because a horse needs to be able to canter pretty well in order to perform such work safely and to good effect. The warning given about trying to force improvement in trot applies, to a greater degree. However, once a horse can canter in good rhythm and balance, properly conducted periods of gymnastic jumping will add variety to his work and help improve strength, suppleness and impulsion. Riders who want to carry out gymnas-tic jumping exercises are advised to seek properly experienced assistance in the construction of grids, and should be mindful that multiple jumping efforts are physically quite demanding of the horse.

---

[4] Some of the conformation faults noted, and a tendency to run in trot, may be prevalent in horses bred primarily for draught work. It is interesting to note that, in the late nineteenth/early twentieth century, certain French equestrian authorities (who trained many horses bred primarily for trotting) recommended and practised walk to canter transitions, to the virtual exclusion of walk to trot.

·8·

TRANSITIONS

A transition is simply a change from one gait to another, either upward to a faster gait, or downward to a slower one. A direct transition is one which misses out an intermediate gait (or gaits) – for example, halt to canter, or canter to walk. A progressive transition is one in which there are a few strides of the intermediate gait – for example, in a progressive transition from canter to walk, you would ride three or four strides of trot before walking. In the early stages of training, all transitions should be progressive, because a young horse will have neither the understanding nor the physical development to perform direct transitions correctly. This general precept also applies to older horses whose level of schooling is limited and/or who require remedial schooling. It is noteworthy that, in Preliminary and Novice Level dressage tests, the requirements to perform direct transitions are very limited.

A good transition – of any sort – is smooth, with the horse remaining calm, obedient and balanced, and immediately adopting a good rhythm in the new gait. Although the primary purpose of a transition is to change from one gait to another, performed correctly, transitions play a valuable role in improving the horse's balance and engagement, as we shall see in due course.

PRINCIPLES OF RIDING TRANSITIONS

The most important thing to understand about transitions is that they are *all* about going forwards. In a downward transition, you do not want to think in terms of 'coming back to ...', for the very good reason that you do not want the horse to 'come back' anywhere; you want him to keep going forwards, but in a different gait. When, for example, you ride a transition from canter to trot, your aids should be saying to the horse 'Keep going forwards, but do so in trot'. Similarly, when you are preparing for an upward transition, although you must be aware of the need for the existing gait to be active, you should not think in terms of having to go faster. The horse does not need to go faster *in order* to perform an upward transition; he will do so *as a result* of the upward transition. (This, fundamentally, is why he moves in different gaits.)

Another important point about transitions is that they are prime examples of the need to find the most effective way of using the aids to communicate with an individual horse at a particular time (as discussed in Chapter 2). A prime example of this is the transition from trot to canter – a transition from the simplest gait to a much more complex one, with the added necessity of choosing a leading leg. With a young or novice horse, who is just learning to canter on the required lead, the appropriate aids may be to open the inside rein a little and to give fairly firm leg aids, the outside leg drawn back somewhat to signal that the horse should strike off with his outside hind, and both legs giving the forward-driving aid. The reason for this is that, at this stage, the horse needs obvious signals to establish correct bend and to lead with the correct leg. However, as he becomes more supple, balanced, experienced and attentive, these aids can be gradually refined until he will take the correct canter lead from much lighter aids.

As we saw in Chapter 2, this process of gradual refinement should apply to all aids. In the context of transitions, progress will be assisted if there is proper preparation before the transition is requested. There are two simple reasons for this. First, correct preparation will alert the horse to the fact that something is about to be asked of him and second, this same preparation will make it easier for him to respond. This brings us to consider the actual phases of a transition.

THE PHASES OF A TRANSITION

In any transition there are three basic phases: prepare; ask; allow. Because a transition is a direct product of the gait from which it is made, it is unlikely that it will be of better quality than that gait[1]. So, in preparation for a transition, you should first ensure that the horse is moving actively and attentively, and that he is straight if on a straight line, or correctly bent if on a curve. You should also prepare yourself with a momentary mental check of your posture, and ensure that you have a clear idea of where you want the transition to take place.

The moment before you ask for a transition, it is helpful to apply a gentle half-halt (see Chapter 6) – just enough to say to the horse 'Listen, we're going to do something different'[2]. The aids should then be applied clearly and without fuss (the 'ask' phase) *out* of half-halt for an upward transition and as a *continuation* for a downward transition.

Once you have asked for a transition, you must allow the horse to respond. That is to say, you must not do anything that makes it hard for him to obey you. For example, if you have asked the horse to go forward into an upward transition, allow him to do so. If you gave rather too strong a leg aid, and the horse surged into trot or canter, do not respond by hauling on the reins – this will destroy the quality of the new gait, not improve it. Instead, accept your own error and allow a few strides in which to make a gradual improvement in rhythm and balance.

The other thing you should do once the horse has responded to your request for a transition is stop asking; your seat, legs and hands should remain in quiet communication with the horse until you need to send another specific signal. As we saw in The Principles of Applying the Aids (Don't Nag) in Chapter 2, it is

confusing to keep asking the horse to do something he has already done and, in this case, it may not *allow* him to obey you. If, for example, you keep the aids on too long after a canter to trot transition, the horse may think you want him to walk. If he does so, it is not he who is at fault!

AIDS FOR BASIC UPWARD AND DOWNWARD TRANSITIONS

As we have just seen, the *precise* aids for any transition may vary slightly from horse to horse and in accord with an individual horse's level of training. However, *in principle*, the aids for all upward transitions are very similar and so are the aids for all downward transitions. This is not surprising because, in every case, the rider is asking the horse to move either up or down a gait.

To ride an upward transition, the basic aids are a slight driving effect from the seat (see Chapter 2), together with increased leg pressure to give a clearly defined signal, and a softening of the rein contact to allow the horse to respond. The seat and leg should act fractionally before the hands soften – as you feel yourself give the seat and legs aid, the hands ease. In all these essential respects, the aids for an upward transition to canter are the same as for those to trot; the canter aids are applied asymmetrically simply to signal which leg you want the horse to lead with.

There is a major potential difference between upward and downward transitions, which is the main reason why downward transitions are more difficult to ride well. Because the horse is 'rear-engined', any upward transition, ridden more or less correctly, will initially produce a little more engagement of the hindquarters. (Whether this level of engagement can be maintained in the new gait will depend on the rider's skill.) However,

• *Upward transitions from halt to walk (above), walk to trot (middle) and trot to canter (below).*

---

[1] If it was entirely down to the rider, one might say that a transition can never be better than the gait that precedes it. However, experienced horses, on being asked for a transition, will sometimes adjust their own activity/balance to make the transition easier for themselves. This generosity on the horse's part should not be abused or taken for granted by the rider.
[2] There is an old axiom that one should never surprise the horse with the aids for a transition.

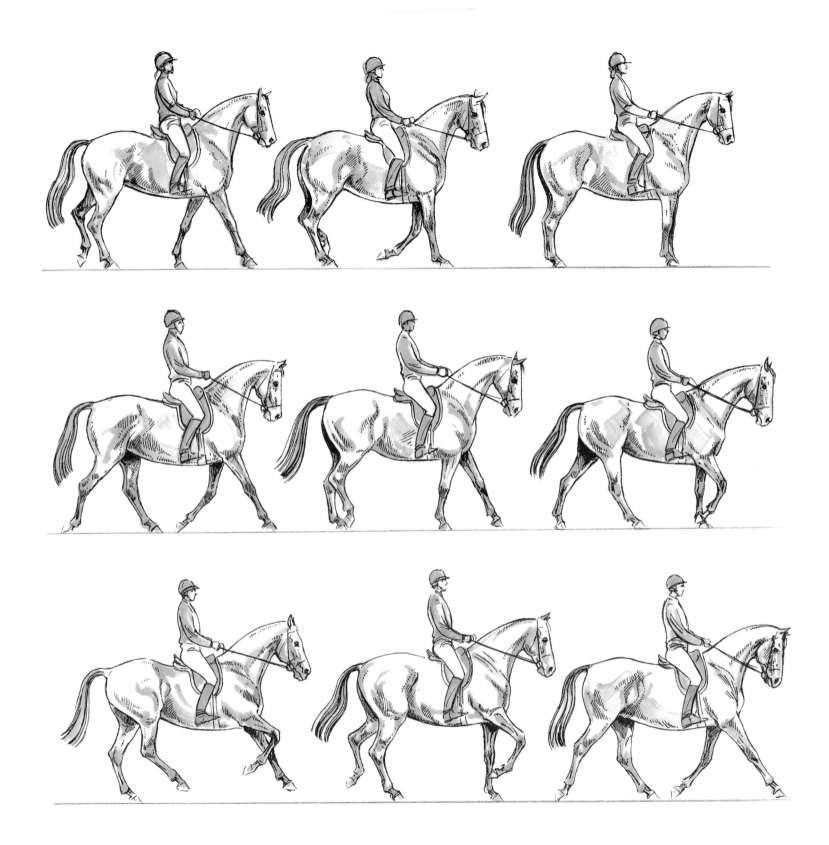

in downward transitions, the horse has a fundamental choice whether to act like a machine or a horse – and his decision will be largely influenced by how he is ridden. When a mechanical [...] decelerates, the laws of physics tip its nose downward. If [...] done an emergency stop in a car, you will know [...] In any stop, other than a complete gliding to a [...] some dipping of the bonnet. When a horse, [...] object, decelerates, he too is subject to the laws [...] he is able to take some action to avoid it [...] too will be tipped forward, onto his forehand. [...] chooses to slow down by bracing his forelegs in a [...], he can actually add to the effect.

[...] the horse, unlike the car, does have the where-[...] this effect of deceleration. He has the option to [...] himself by moving the levers of his hind limbs more [...] himself, so that, by carrying more of his weight to [...] counteracts the tipping forward forces of deceleration. [...] during downward transitions, the rider has the [...] between the horse finishing the transition on his fore-[...] finishing it in balance. What can be done to influence [...] come?

[...] the first outcome is very simple – you just pull on [...] reins. A downward transition produced mainly from the [...] will have the same effect as braking hard in your car. The [...]'s weight will tip forward, and the horse will arrive in the [...] gait on his forehand, with his hindquarters disengaged. [...] is guaranteed. Achieving the second outcome is more [...] cult, but it carries great rewards. We mean this not just [...] the sense of producing a good transition, but because it is [...] dence of a real ability to have the horse on the aids and to [...] luence and control the horse's hindquarters.

[...] If we are to ask the horse for a transition in which he retains [...] balance by stepping more underneath himself, we are talking [...] out a transition that asks for more engagement. Using the [...] *more* presupposes that he already has *some*. This brings us [...] ck to the need to prepare for a transition; the need to ensure [...] t the horse is moving with reasonable activity, in reasonable

Downward transitions from walk to halt (above), trot to walk [...]dle) and canter to trot (below).

balance, before we ask for the change of gait. It also brings us back to the idea of using a half-halt, and the phrase used earlier, that the downward transition should be ridden as a *continuation* of the half-halt. This is the crux of the matter. As we saw earlier (Chapter 6) the half-halt is, in itself, a momentary action, the aids being eased as soon as they have achieved their rebalancing effect. However, if these same aids are applied with slightly more emphasis and are sustained for a little longer, they can have the effect of literally collecting and balancing the horse into the new gait. (This is especially obvious in the transition from canter to trot, where there is a distinct choice between engaging and balancing the canter until the horse can move effortlessly into trot, or inducing him to fall out of canter into an unbalanced, running trot.) To reiterate the basic aids, the rider uses seat and legs to 'compress' the horse slightly into restraining ('holding', *not pulling*) hands. The horse increases the engagement of his hind limbs, which allows him to remain in balance as he decelerates in response to the aids – sustained a little longer than for the half-halt – and then 'drops down a gear' into the new gait. As he does so, these specific aids are eased and the horse is encouraged *forwards* in the new gait. As ever, we emphasise the need to think forwards but, in some contexts, this is extremely significant after a downward transition. If, for example, you have acquired a horse (perhaps from a riding school) who has been ridden by a lot of novices, he may have developed the notion that any downward transition (but especially into walk) is an invitation for inactivity that may extend to sprouting roots. With such horses, it is essential to really pick up the first strides of the new gait with positive aids. If this is done consistently, the horse should soon abandon the habit, which is often rooted in boredom and confusion.

The one aid that we should discuss further in the context of downward transitions is the use of the seat. As mentioned in Chapter 2, the driving seat needs to be clearly understood and used with prudence. The footnote explains that, applied crudely and overdone, this aid will drive the horse into a hollow outline which, amongst other effects, makes it impossible for the horse to engage. Such an aid could have no place in the type of downward transition just described. The initial seat aid used to encourage the 'compression' of the horse must be effective, but it must be more subtle than this. A useful mental picture might be the difference between pushing with your hand gently on someone's back to encourage them into action, and jabbing them with a pitchfork.

To develop this theme, there is an adjustment of the seat that can be useful when riding downward transitions on young horses, those with otherwise weak backs, or those who are hollow-backed. This requires some 'feel' and timing, but it can help to produce an element of rounding and engagement that these horses might not otherwise offer. (Remember, such horses may be at a stage where only the very rudiments of engagement can be expected.) In the first place, with such horses, the rider's seat will, as standard, be a shade lighter than on a more robust horse whose schooling is more advanced. Therefore, when the aids for the downward transition are first applied, rather than actively pushing, the rider's seat will be 'holding' (the weight spread pretty evenly over the buttocks and thighs, with the lower back and stomach muscles firm). As the rider senses that the horse is about to make the transition, the seat is lightened a fraction (a little more weight is taken on the thighs), thus encouraging the horse to step under. As with many other aspects of training, this accommodation of the horse's physical state can be modified in parallel with his physical development.

DIRECT TRANSITIONS

There is no fundamental difference between how progressive transitions and direct transitions are ridden. Basically, direct transitions are a case of more of the same; the aim being to give signals which the horse can understand to mean 'change up or down, but miss one (or two) gaits'. However, if we consider the aids just described for basic transitions from one gait to the next, we can see quite clearly that expanding these aids to tell the horse to miss out a gait will make bigger demands of the horse. In the first place, it presupposes that the horse has a good under-standing of the aids for progressive transitions, will be able to interpret the fact that he is being asked for something different, and will have some idea of what this something different is. In the second place, it presupposes that he has developed sufficient balance, suppleness and strength to respond to these increased

demands (especially in the downward transitions) in a broadly correct manner. Therefore, it is pointless starting work on direct transitions until the horse can move consistently well in the working gaits, and can make consistently satisfactory trans[...] between one gait and the next.

The other point to consider is that, because d[...] are asking for a bigger effect, any mistakes in t[...] ration or application of the aids will be magni[...] especially when schooling at home, you should [...] that the horse is moving well before asking for [...] and avoid making a hurried or ill-prepared transiti[...] sake of it.

Direct upward transitions are, among other things, [...] exercises in obedience and attentiveness and as a chec[...] horse is on the aids. If he is, then they are reasonably [...] forward. From halt to trot, apply rather more leg press[...] if you were asking for walk. For walk to canter, ensure [...] walk is active but unhurried, then apply your usual can[...] clearly and distinctly. If you can feel it, you should give t[...] as the horse's outside hind leg is stepping forward unde[...] him. If you cannot do so, you may have to apply the aid[...] wait a moment, because he cannot give you the correct[...] until his legs are in the right position[3]. So long as the ho[...] active in walk, and really understands the canter aids, wal[...] canter should pose few problems.

When introducing direct upward transitions, it is import[...] to avoid thinking 'I've got to get through to the horse at [...] cost' and giving aids that are frantic, rather than just firm a[...] distinct. If the horse understands these unnecessarily strong ai[...] he will run or surge into the new gait and, if he does not und[...] stand them, he will just run forward in a state of confusion[...] the initial aids are not quite distinct enough, it is probable th[...] the horse will 'think about it' but, being rather undecided abo[...]

• *Direct upward transitions from halt to trot (above) and walk [...]*
canter (below). Proper preparation and distinct – not frantic – ai[...]
are required.

[3] The former is much more desirable. The process of feeling the movement in walk[...] discussed in Chapter 7.

vehicl

you have

this to be

*h*alt, you wil

*be*ing a movin

of *p*hysics. Unl

hap*pe*ning, he

Indee*d,* if he

braking *actio*

However

withal to *d*

rebalance

underneat

the rear, h

There

choice

hand, o

the ou

Ack

the re

reins

hors

new

Tha

diff

in

evi

inf

his

ab

te

ba

tha

• D

(*mi*

sitions

ransitions
der's prepa-
d. Therefore,
always ensure
the transition,
on just for the

useful as
k that the
straight-
ure than
that the
ter aids
he aids
rneath
's and
lead
se is
k to

ant
ny
nd
ds,
er-
If
at
ut

to
ds

was

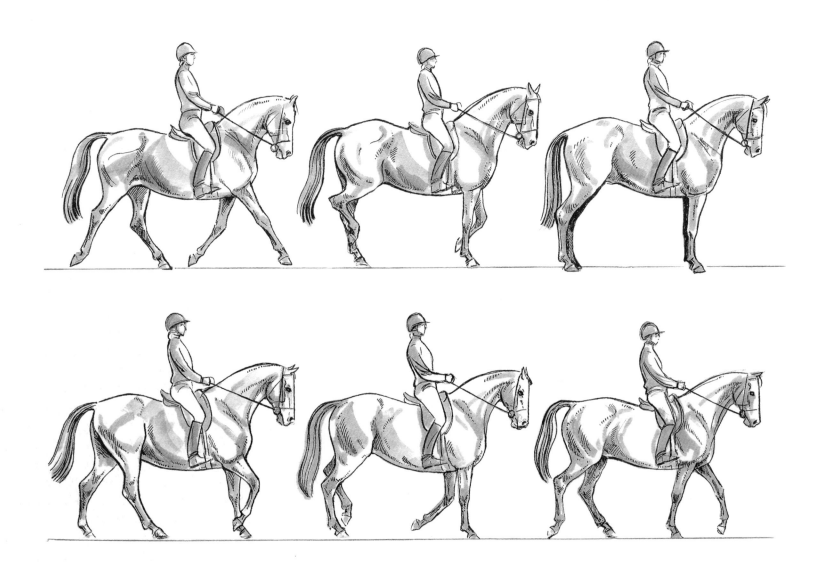

what is being asked of him, not quite go through with the change. In this case, rather than fiddling about and nagging, just re-establish the existing gait and ask again, a little more clearly, and you should find that the penny will soon drop.

Direct downward transitions (except, perhaps, trot to halt) really belong to a more advanced stage of training than is dealt with in this book. Generally speaking, they require a degree of engagement and aid coordination towards which horse and rider will progress by correct attention to basic work. Arbitrary attempts to ride, for example, canter to halt transitions out of the blue would suggest a rider who has spent too much time watching cowboy films, and too little time studying the idea of progressive training. However, riders who want to start working towards direct downward transitions might consider the following points.

When you do introduce direct downward transitions, begin with (sitting) trot to halt (halting is dealt with shortly). While you should aim to make the transition at a selected marker, you should give preference to a smooth transition which is a little late rather than an 'emergency stop' at the marker. Since you will be more used to timing your aids from walk, it may take a little practice to give the horse sufficient warning to stop correctly at a marker from trot. Similarly, if you get the timing or coordination of the aids wrong, or if the horse doesn't quite understand, it is better to accept a transition that includes a step or two of walk than to sense that the horse is about to walk, drive him back into trot and then attempt a late, abrupt halt while the horse is still responding to your forward driving aids.

Do not attempt canter to walk until you are proficient at trot to walk *and* your horse can canter with his hocks well underneath him, in good balance and rhythm. In the early stages of riding canter to walk, while you do not want the canter inactive, think in terms of 'soft and steady'. Do not, at first, worry too much about where the transition is to take place, instead, allow yourself plenty of time and gradually move the back end of the horse up into gently containing hands, until he can go into

• *Direct downward transitions from trot to halt (above) and canter to walk (below). These transitions should only be introduced once the horse has reached an appropriate stage in his training (see text).*

a balanced walk. Again, if at first he needs to take a stride or two of trot, do not fight this. Good direct downward transitions require patience and practice; impatience and tolerance will *create* problems, not solve them.

COMMON FAULTS IN TRANSITIONS

As we have seen, a transition is largely a product of the gait from which it is made. Therefore, defects in the preceding gait will very probably be reflected in the transition itself.

1. Preceding gait inactive. The transition will be sluggish and imprecise. The horse will 'fall' into a downward transition.

2. Preceding gait hurried. The horse will run into (or instead of performing) an upward transition. He will resist, then 'come back' into an unbalanced downward transition.

3. Horse inattentive prior to transition. If he is not listening then, in one way or another, the transition will be imprecise. In a test, there is the possibility of the rider being panicked into giving incorrect aids and getting an even worse transition than would otherwise have been the case.

4. Horse crooked in preceding gait. This will cause the transition to be crooked and perhaps unbalanced. This is a particular problem in transitions to and from canter. If the horse is crooked to the outside in an upward transition, he may take the wrong lead. For a downward transition, his hind legs will not be aligned correctly, so it will be both crooked and unbalanced.

The cure for these faults lies in avoiding, or putting right, the deficiency in the gait before the transition is made. Faults in the transitions themselves arise from errors in giving the aids. These may be related to faulty posture, or they may point to the need for better communication – in particular, the rider being more aware of feedback from the horse. It is always worth remembering that the horse not doing exactly what you want doesn't necessarily mean that he is not listening to you – it may be that he is listening very intently, but you are not sending the right message!

TRANSITIONS IN TESTS

The main difference between riding transitions in tests and riding them when training is that, in tests, there is an obligation to perform them at certain times and places. We will explore this issue further in the final chapter. For the time being, we will consider one aspect of basic level tests which, to some extent, mirrors the training philosophy of riding transitions when best prepared to do so.

In many of the basic level tests, it is permissible to ride certain transitions between markers, rather than at a marker (for example, the test sheet will say 'Between H and C...', rather than 'at C'). In such circumstances, it is sensible to plan to ride transitions just after the first marker. This gives you an extra moment or two for preparation if the existing gait is unsatisfactory, and lessens the risk of riding an abrupt or late transition in order to fit it in, which might occur if you planned to ride the transition almost on the second marker. Also, if everything does go to plan, and you make a smooth transition near the first marker, you will have slightly more time in which to concentrate upon the next movement. However, if your horse has difficulty taking a particular canter lead and the test requires you to canter between two markers that form a corner, it can be helpful to apply the aids just as you are moving through the corner when, hopefully, the horse will be correctly bent and in the best position to take the correct lead. Also, in an enclosed arena (such as an indoor school), consider giving the canter aid going into the corner if the horse tends to rush, or coming out of it if he tends to be a little inactive.

THE HALT

The halt is included in this chapter because achieving halt necessarily requires a downward transition, and departing from it requires an upward transition. A good halt is accurate (in the right place), straight and square, with the horse remaining on the aids, attentive and still. A correct halt can be thought of as the horse standing to attention rather than simply stopping. In this respect, it can be helpful for the rider to think of halt as simply a pause in forward movement, or even as a preparation for the next movement.

Since riding into halt is a downward transition, it is likely to be performed best from an active, balanced gait, in which the horse is moving as straight as possible. By 'active' we do not mean that the horse should be prepared to halt by being driven strongly forward, but that he should be showing enough activity to allow him to step *forward* into a square, balanced

• *A correct halt: square and attentive.*

halt. Although, by definition, halting requires the cessation of actual forward movement, in order to halt correctly, the horse must maintain a *willingness* to move forward. This plays an important role both in establishing the halt and in moving off.

The other point relating to halt as a downward transition is that, like other downward transitions, it makes sense to establish the progressive, gait by gait transitions to a reasonable standard before attempting the direct transitions. Thus you should ensure that the horse can halt consistently well from walk before starting work on halting directly from the other gaits.

That said, we should mention that, once the horse can perform satisfactory transitions directly from trot to halt, the exercise of riding repeated trot-halt-trot transitions is excellent for improving engagement and building up the horse's hindquarters. This is another example of building the training process block by block.

THE AIDS FOR HALT

To ride a good halt, even from walk, it is necessary to think ahead. Abrupt halts are usually poor ones; the horse needs a little time to respond to your aids, so if you wish to halt from walk at a particular marker, you will need to start applying the aids a horse's length or so before the marker.

Since halt is a downward transition, it follows that the aids will have similarities with other downward transitions. However, there is one significant difference – whereas the other aids signal: 'Please keep going forward but change down a gait', the halt aids must signal: 'Please cease forward movement but remain prepared to start again'. In order to do this, the forward driving aids need to be moderated to an extent where they are just sufficient to encourage the horse to step forward into the halt. The main aids must be those that signal 'stop', because that is what the horse is required to do. We have mentioned before the idea of horse and rider mirroring each other's movement, and this idea can be usefully employed in halting. One way of explaining this is that *you* think about stopping, and the horse stops. This may sound rather esoteric, but it is entirely consistent with the correct mechanisms for applying the aids. What happens is this. You have the horse in an active walk, on the aids. You intend to halt at a certain marker. As you approach the marker,

you form a strong mental picture that *you* – shoulders, back, hips and heels – will stop at the marker. With this intention, you firm up your upper body, 'lock' your hips and close your thighs on the saddle, as though to block further forward movement. The horse halts. Why? Because the more or less subconscious actions of your body have given him signals to do so. In firming up your upper body, you will have moved your shoulders back a fraction, which will have had the effect of slightly increasing the rein contact (without any overt backward movement of your hands). The slight bracing of your lower back will have resulted in your seat gently pushing the horse forwards into this contact. The whole firming of your upper body and blocking actions of your thighs will send a signal of inertia to the horse, which will be substantially different from the sensations he gets when you are actively encouraging forward movement. He is no longer being given any incentive to move forwards, but is being given signals to stop.

We would emphasise that these aids have nothing in common with the antic of leaning back and pulling on the reins: they are about stepping the horse up into still hands, and holding him there with a firm, erect body.

Generally speaking, once a horse has completed a transition, the rider should cease giving the specific aids that requested it. If it is the intention that the halt, once established, should be maintained for any length of time, the aids can be fractionally eased. However, it should be remembered that the requirement in this case is for the horse to remain in halt – in this respect, the halt can be seen as a kind of frozen transition. There are, of course, times (such as waiting at a busy road junction) when it may be necessary for the horse to remain immobile for some while, and he must be taught to do so when necessary. However, in a schooling context, it is usually better to keep halts fairly brief, so that the horse remains attentive and ready to move off again. (As we shall see shortly, brief halts can also be useful in addressing problems.)

COMMON FAULTS IN HALT

Halting too early or late. If the halt is otherwise good, this is simply a case of mistiming the aids. As with the timing of all transitions, this can be improved by better preparation and more

(a)

(b)

(c)

(d)

practice. In the short term, bear in mind that, in a test, a good halt a little off the marker will score better than a poor one on the marker.

Halt crooked; the horse halts askew. This can result from crooked movement before the halt, or uneven aids, in which case the cures are better preparation or aid applications respectively. Uneven aids are sometimes applied by riders who unconsciously use one hand more strongly than the other, inducing a crooked-ness in the horse's body that they then try to correct with their legs. An even, but over-strong rein contact can also cause crookedness because the horse may try to evade it by swinging his quarters to one side (usually to his 'hollow' side). Where crookedness is created or provoked by such aids, the rider should try to apply aids more in line with those just discussed. It has to be said, however, that a horse who is markedly crooked in his natural pose and movement is very likely to reflect this in his halts, until such time as this crookedness is reduced by remedial training (see Chapter 6).

Horse resistant to halt. This may be associated with the over-strong rein aids described above. As well as, or instead of, swinging his quarters out, the horse may hollow his back, poke his nose and trail his hindquarters. The cure is to apply the aids correctly and more gently. In some cases, a horse may also resist the halt for reasons of over-excitement or disobedience described below.

Halt not established. The horse is never really still; he fidgets and squirms about and may try to move forward, backward or side-ways. This can happen if the horse is over-excited or disobedient. If it happens in a test, there is not much you can do at the time – although it is better to stay calm and quiet than to get flustered and react by pulling the horse about. The real solution is more schooling at home and/or familiarising the horse with strange environments. When schooling, the best procedure is to

• *Incorrect versions of halt. (a) Not square; (b) hollow outline, with hocks trailing; (c) not square behind, and crooked; (d) crooked, reflecting rider's aids and posture.*

insist upon, and reward, brief halts, gradually increasing the duration as the horse begins to comply. This is far better than getting into prolonged battles, which may provoke you into using the aids incorrectly and are likely to make the problem worse. Sometimes, however, a fidgety horse is simply reacting to harsh aids from a tense, nervous rider. In this case, it is up to the rider to try and relax and apply the aids correctly.

Halt not square. The horse halts fairly straight, but not with a foot at each corner. If this is very obvious, (as though the horse had simply frozen in mid-stride), either the preceding walk was not active enough, or the aids were imprecise. These faults can be cured by riding more positively (but still correctly). However, some horses will habitually halt with one foot a little out of alignment, most commonly leaving a particular hind foot trailing. Although this may be related to one-sidedness, if the halt is pretty well correct in other respects, it can be seen in this context as habit, rather than a substantial flaw. Astute trainers who note this trait in a young horse will act to prevent it from developing, but if you acquire a horse who has been doing it for years it is probably best to accept that, because it *is* now a habit, it can only be cured by patience and persistence. Unless you are confident that you can feel when, and how much, a leg is trailing, a knowledgeable assistant on the ground, who can see what you are trying to feel, can be a great help; failing this, a mirror in an indoor school can provide a valuable point of reference. These aids are much preferable to trying to look down and to the rear, which may unbalance the horse, disturb the halt you have attained and muddy the overall picture.

The basic cure for a trailing hind leg is to use your own leg on the same side to ask the horse to move his leg forwards. If it seems necessary to reinforce your leg aid with a schooling whip, both should be applied together. Both leg and whip should be used with discretion, to avoid any over-reaction on the horse's part that might exacerbate the overall problem. You do not want a strong leg aid that will encourage the horse to step sideways, away from it, nor a whip aid that will cause the horse to step forward. As with so many aids, timing, rather than force, is of key importance. In this case, the aid to square up should be

● *Correct forms of salute for female and male riders.*

applied *the moment that forward movement ceases*, if the offending leg is deemed to be trailing. Obviously, if a particular halt is square, this additional aid should not be given. If, however, the moment is missed and the horse establishes a halt that is not square, it is better to accept the fact, move off and try again. At this stage, fiddling about or trying to resolve the situation with too strong an aid will just confuse and irritate the horse, to no positive effect.

During the period of correcting the habit, square halts should be praised and rewarded; those that are not square should receive a mild verbal admonishment. This admonishment should be accompanied by moving off promptly and, as soon as active movement is established, trying again. Indeed, one ploy that may help to eliminate this fault is to trot off briskly after each halt. In order to do this, the horse will have to move any lagging leg quickly into position in order to be able to push off. The idea is that, if the halt to trot transition is repeated on numerous occasions, the horse may come to think of the halt not as a rest period in which he can stand anyhow, but as a preparation to trot. If this succeeds then, in addition to learning to halt square, the horse is also learning to halt in an engaged, attentive manner, ready to respond to any demand for forward movement.[4]

THE SALUTE

In dressage tests, the halt at the start (if any) and finish of the test is accompanied by a salute. This is an integral part of the test, and must be performed. Essentially a courteous acknowledgement of the judge, it also shows whether the rider has control of the halt. Originally a military style movement, the salute has been modified somewhat down the years. The method currently in use for all junior riders, female riders, and males wearing a hat with a chin strap is as follows: upon halting, the reins and whip (if carried) are taken in one hand; the free hand is lowered to the rider's side; the rider nods to the judge. Male riders who are wearing an unsecured hat should remove it and lower it in the free hand. Upon completion of the halt, the rider should move smoothly and unhurriedly forward into the required gait.

To perform a good salute, which conveys the impression of being in control, you must first establish a halt with the horse properly on the aids. Transferring the reins to one hand must then be done carefully, so that the rein contact is disturbed as little as possible. If you intend to compete, it makes sense to practise salutes on a fairly regular basis, once the basic halts have been established to a good standard.

[4] Once the desired effect is achieved, halt to walk transitions should be interspersed with halt to trot, to avoid anticipation becoming ingrained.

·9·

GAIT VARIATIONS AND OTHER WORK AT NOVICE LEVEL

In this chapter we will look at various aspects of work that is included in dressage tests at Novice Level[1] for – we would suggest – one of two reasons. These are, first to check that the training so far has been along correct lines and second, to offer signposts for the way forward. The inclusion of the latter is, in effect, sending the message 'Consider introducing this work in preparation for the next stage of training'. As hinted at earlier, this message should be received and acted upon sensibly. All new work should be incorporated gradually, at a time that is appropriate to an individual horse's progress. Once this work is established to a reasonable level, it is reasonable – if you so wish – to enter a competition that requires it. Trying to introduce new work in a hurry, on the basis that 'they're doing Novice 39 down the road next Sunday', invites an under-prepared, panicky and forceful performance, which will not, in the horse's terms, serve as a positive introduction to the new work.

The movements that we view primarily as training checks are free walk on a long rein and the giving and re-taking of the rein. Those that we view primarily as signposts to the way forward are lengthened strides, counter-canter and rein-back.

FREE WALK ON A LONG REIN

This movement is a derivation of medium walk. From this basic gait, the rider continues to ask the horse to move forwards in an active walk, without bustling him, and gradually and

smoothly opens the fingers, lightening the hold on the reins and offering the horse the opportunity to take the contact forward and down. In a good free walk on a long rein the horse remains

• The correct beginnings of free walk on a long rein. The rider is offering the rein and the horse is starting to stretch his head and neck forward and down. The steps remain long and active, but unhurried.

[1] Or other country's equivalent levels.

• *Incorrect free walk on a long rein: the horse has been held up and constricted by the rider's hands; when given the rein, he falls onto the forehand.*

• *Incorrect free walk on a long rein. The rider throws away the contact and gives clumsy driving aids; the horse goes into a half-hearted trot.*

• *Incorrect free walk on a long rein. When offered the rein, the horse puts his head up – a sign that he is not being encouraged to work over his topline in his general training.*

in balance and obedient to the aids. He retains his rhythm in walk and continues to step out at least to the extent of tracking up. He should accept the offer to stretch his head and neck forward and down, gently taking the bit down with a relaxed jaw.

As an indication of training, free walk is just as valuable at home as it is in a test, and it can be used at intervals between other work, and at the end of a training session, for this purpose. Correct free walk can also be used as the gait of relaxation, because it combines a continued (though not stressful) degree of activity with a chance for the horse to stretch the muscles of his topline.

COMMON FAULTS IN FREE WALK ON A LONG REIN

As mentioned, poor performance often points to deficiencies in overall training, rather than relating simply to how the movement is ridden.

1. When the rein is offered, the horse tips onto his forehand and takes shorter, hurried steps. This indicates that he was previously being held up by the rider's hands, rather than balancing himself.

2. The horse runs into trot. This may be evidence that he was being restrained in walk by the rider's hands (that is, he was not submissive). On the other hand, it may be that the rider gave very clumsy aids for the free walk; suddenly 'throwing away' the rein contact and giving the horse a dig in the ribs is highly likely to cause this reaction.

3. The walk becomes less active. This may be because some of the horse's previous activity was fuelled by a desire to escape a harsh rein contact; this is especially likely if the preceding walk was short-striding and tense. On the other hand, it may be that the horse is frequently allowed to plod about on a long rein when out hacking. Although horses should sometimes be allowed to relax when out hacking, there is a distinct difference between proper free walk on a long rein and aimless meandering. The latter should not be encouraged, first, because this is when they are most likely to stumble or shy violently and second, because it is important that the general *quality* of the gait is preserved.

4. The horse does not stretch his neck, or he puts his head *up*. This is a sign that, in his general training, he is not encouraged to stretch his topline. He is likely to be tight, tense, restricted in front by the rider and perhaps even hollow-backed. These serious flaws must be remedied by appropriate training (see Chapter 6).

• *A smooth and unhurried transition from free walk, through a few steps of medium walk, into working trot.*

NOTES FOR TESTS

Except when it occurs at the end of a test, free walk on a long rein is often followed (on the test sheet) by an immediate instruction to perform a change of gait. For example, the test might require free walk across a long diagonal, then trot at the quarter marker. It is not feasible to make such a transition abruptly and well so, in the last few strides of free walk, you should gently and smoothly regain the required length of rein, returning to medium walk before attempting the change of gait. The necessity to do this will be understood by the judge.

When a test requires the free walk to be performed on a half-circle, this will show up any tendency for the rider to steer the horse on the circle with the reins (and the extent to which the horse expects this.) As we shall see in the next chapter, such aids are not appropriate to circle work. Therefore, if the circle work and the free walk are basically correct, this movement should provide no problems.

GIVE AND RE-TAKE THE REINS

This exercise, which is commonly performed at canter, requires the rider to 'push both hands forward to release the contact and then re-take it. This should be one continuous movement'.

The purpose of the exercise is to demonstrate that the horse is balancing himself – not leaning on the rider's hands. Success or failure depends almost entirely upon whether this is so – in other words, upon the quality of the gait immediately before the movement is performed. If the horse is in balance, the movement, done correctly and smoothly, is quite straightforward. You simply maintain your existing seat and leg aids and move your hands in the prescribed fashion – the horse will retain balance, outline and rhythm. If, however, he was being restrained or propped up by your hands, he will run or fall onto the forehand. Thus, what this movement demonstrates is more important than the movement itself and it is valuable to practise it

at home. If you experience any problem, you should look seriously at your basic schooling. Are you riding the horse too much 'on the hands'; are you pre-occupied with forcing him into an outline? Why is he not engaging his hindquarters and carrying himself in a basic degree of balance? Because these questions are so fundamental, there is little point in trying to introduce

• *Giving the reins in canter: the horse stays in balance and keeps his outline.*

(a)

new work until they are addressed and progress is made on the remedy. There is little point, either, in trying to compete – simply choosing a test which does not require this movement would be an evasion of the first order.

At the time of writing, there is one movement at Novice Level that is something of a cross between the principles of free walk and the giving and re-taking of the reins. This is performed from working trot. The requirement is to begin a 20 m circle then to 'allow the horse to take the rein and stretch', the rider re-establishing normal rein contact in the last couple of strides of the circle. Again, this is a demonstration of whether the basic qualities of rhythm, activity and balance are instilled in the horse's trot, and whether horse and rider can perform a circle without undue reliance on the reins. The remarks already made about the related movements are equally applicable here, including the value of trying the exercise at home.

LENGTHENED STRIDES IN TROT AND CANTER

Lengthening the stride is the first step towards the medium and extended gaits and, as such, it can be seen as pointing the way forward for horses whose training can advanceto these levels. However, it also has a role in checking training to date, since the successful introduction of this work will depend largely upon the quality of the working gaits and upon the rider's ability to really communicate with the horse.

(b)

• Giving and re-taking the reins will show up the horse's training.
(a) Here, the horse has hollowed his outline and run on, suggesting that the rider had been holding him in a false outline and balance.
(b) Here, the rider is out of position and the horse has fallen onto the forehand.

So far as tests are concerned, most require that you 'show some lengthened strides'. The actual number is not specified, nor is the precise degree of lengthening. This is because, at this stage, the judge is simply looking for evidence that the horse can, when requested, show a distinct change in stride length out of the working gait, and can return to it smoothly and in balance. These, of course, are the criteria that you should seek in work at home.

At Novice Level there are also a few tests that make limited demands for medium trot and canter. These are more specific than simple lengthening. These medium gaits are characterised by a consistent and significant lengthening beyond the working gaits (with over-tracking, typically, by a couple of hoofprints), coupled with an expressive roundness that comes from correct use of the horse's supple back. In order to produce correct medium trot and canter, the horse must be supple, substantially straight and capable of showing a significant degree of engagement and free forward movement. These are qualities that will hopefully be seen in a horse specifically selected and trained for competition dressage, and the inclusion of medium work in Novice Level tests may be seen as a signpost for their riders. Many other horses – especially those with less athletic conformation – may find true medium gaits very demanding and owners of such horses should be wary of asking more than the horse can deliver. In all cases, the horse needs to understand the requirements of basic lengthening before any further demands are made, and it is this basic work that we shall consider.

When lengthening correctly, the horse's *frequency* of stride (number of strides per given period) remains the same, but he covers more ground because he is taking longer steps.

PREPARATION FOR LENGTHENED STRIDES

Before teaching the horse to lengthen his stride in trot, it is sensible to ensure that he will always respond correctly to clear aids for the trot to canter transition. This will lessen the chance of his being confused by the request to lengthen his stride and

• *Lengthening the trot and canter. Note the difference in stride length between working gaits (left) and lengthening (right).*

responding by running into canter. For similar reasons, it is useful to do some work on direct transitions from walk to canter (see Chapter 8), so that the horse does not think of canter as being something he only ever does as a response to being asked something extra when trotting.

Lengthening the stride is a consequence of the hind legs stepping further forward underneath the horse; these longer steps should be mirrored by those of the forelegs. In order for the horse to do this, he must first be moving with some degree of engagement in the working gaits. Until he is doing this consistently, asking him to lengthen on command will be pointless.

It is also important for the rider to be clear about the basic concept of lengthening. When a horse lengthens his stride, he keeps the same *tempo* (number of strides per period) as in the working gait, but the individual strides are longer. *As a consequence of this*, he travels faster – that is, he travels faster *because* he is taking longer strides, not *in order* to do so. Understanding this will help the rider to give aids that are primarily signals for longer steps, rather than simply for speeding up. (Note that the horse can increase speed either by taking longer strides in the same tempo, or by taking more short strides in a faster tempo. The latter, 'running', is the exact opposite of correct lengthening.[2])

THE AIDS FOR LENGTHENING

Initially, the best place to ask for lengthening is the long side of the arena, once you have come through the corner and the horse is straight. The horse should be performing pretty much the best working gait of which he is capable. It is still a good idea to prepare him with a subtle half-halt, to ensure that he is balanced and attentive. The lengthening should then be requested by a progressive intensifying of the aids. This does not mean that you need to take up most of the long side applying them gradually, but it does mean that you should give the horse time to respond. A sudden, clamping-on of harsh aids must certainly be

---

[2] This latter movement, with short, quick strides, has nothing in common with collection. In collected work, the steps are shorter (in terms of how much ground they cover) because all the joints of the limbs are flexed to a greater degree, so that the limbs travel in a rounded, elevated manner, rather than mainly stepping forward. In collected work, the tempo remains the same as in the working gait, and the horse moves more slowly (in miles per hour) because the strides are shorter. They are, however, very energetic and weight-carrying – the antithesis of the scuttling strides of the running horse.

avoided, since this will just startle the horse into running rather than lengthening.

The basic aids for lengthening are to ask for more activity by bracing your lower back a little and, at the same time, increase the pressure from both legs (this does not mean kicking – see next page). If the horse is to lengthen his stride properly, he will need to lengthen his topline a little, so your hands must allow and encourage this. In trot, the horse keeps his head pretty still throughout the stride cycle, so you can simply move your hands forwards a little as you ask for more activity with your seat and legs. In canter, however, the horse's head moves with the stride cycle so, if you were to do the same as at trot, the rein contact would come and go. Therefore, you have to think in more general terms of allowing the horse to stretch his head forward a little more, and of keeping the contact soft throughout the stride cycle.

• *Incorrect attempt at lengthening the trot – horse running away from kicking leg aids and lost contact.*

• *Incorrect attempt at lengthening the trot – driving with the seat but holding with the reins; the horse resists and does not lengthen.*

As with the introduction of all new work, do not expect perfection at the first time of asking. Praise and reward any positive response and – even if the response was very good – ease the aids and return to the working gait after a few strides. Do not wait for the movement to die. If there is very little initial response, do not hammer away with harsher aids, but re-establish the working gait and try again. Ensure that the working gait is really active and try 'compressing' the horse a little with successive half-halts through the corner. As you come out of the corner, ask for the lengthening straight out of the last half-halt, and reward any positive response.

COMMON FAULTS IN LENGTHENING

1. Especially in trot, giving kicking leg aids rather an increased squeezing pressure. Kicking legs will upset the horse, and encourage him to run away from the leg, taking short, hurried strides – exactly the opposite of what is required. In canter, the legs should stay on the horse's sides in 'canter position' and drive in rhythm with the stride.

2. 'Throwing the reins away' – abandoning the rein contact rather than softening it. This will confuse, rather than encourage the horse, and expose any flaws in training and balance. Done in conjunction with kicking legs, when asking for lengthened trot, it may cause the horse to run into canter.

3. Not softening the rein contact at all. Most horses, especially novices, need some fairly obvious encouragement to lengthen their topline. Driving the horse forward without doing this will probably just make him tense and resistant and may make him run along with a stiff back; he is unlikely to lengthen.

RETURNING TO THE WORKING GAIT

This should be done over a period of two or three strides. In conjunction with decreasing the leg pressure, the pushing effect of seat and back should be neutralised, so that these aids 'hold' or steady the horse into the working gait. At the same time, the softened rein contact should be gradually restored to normal. The reins must not predominate in returning to the working gait, since this would cause loss of balance and engagement.

In tests, lengthened strides are most commonly required down a long side of the arena or across a long diagonal. Since the requirement is for 'some' lengthened strides, you should give yourself time and room for the transitions to and from the lengthening; do not start in a panic or run out of room

• *Correct return from lengthened trot to working trot: the seat and back 'hold' rather than driving; the rein contact, softened for lengthening, is quietly restored. The rein aids must not predominate.*

and finish abruptly. Especially on the diagonal, make sure that the horse is straight before you start asking; also, ensure that you have re-established the working gait before you return to the track. These points are equally pertinent when schooling at home.

At the time of writing, there is one Novice Level test that requires some lengthened strides of canter on a 20 m half-circle. To perform this movement successfully, it will be necessary to take care in establishing the first stride or two of the half-circle (see next chapter). It will also be necessary to ensure that, while the aids for lengthening are applied, they retain their dual function of channelling the horse correctly on a circle: if the driving effect overrides the channelling effect, there is a risk that the horse may be pushed off the half-circle almost on a tangent. It should be evident that a movement such as this should not be attempted until the horse performs good circles in working canter *and* is established in lengthening on a straight line.

● *Incorrect return from lengthened canter to working canter. (a) Rider uses strong leg aids to drive horse into heavy hands, but (b) horse resists and loses rhythm.*

(a)

(b)

● *Incorrect return from lengthened canter to working canter. Rider takes legs off horse's sides and pulls on reins, causing horse to fall into a running trot.*

• *Counter-canter. This horse is cantering on the right lead, but it is clear from the arena boards that he is travelling anti-clockwise (on the left rein).*

COUNTER-CANTER

Counter-canter is when the horse moves in one direction while cantering, as requested by the rider, on the other lead (for example, he circles to the left in right-lead canter). Counter-canter was originally devised as a way of dealing with crookedness, which is often accentuated in the canter. If, for example, the old-time trainers encountered a horse who was concave in right-lead canter, so that his hindquarters turned towards the centre of the arena on that rein, they simply rode on the right lead while cantering round the arena to the left, using the solid walls of the arena to mould the horse into straightness.

Counter-canter remains a useful tool for alleviating crookedness and for making the horse laterally supple. It also plays a role in the development of collection and in preparation for flying changes, and it demonstrates the horse's obedience and the rider's correct use of the aids. It appears, to a very limited extent, in a few Novice Level tests, where it may be seen to have the dual role of pointing the way towards future work and a demonstrating the existing harmony between horse and rider.

Counter-canter should not be attempted until the horse will consistently give the correct (true) lead on both reins, and can sustain a consistently good working canter on both leads. If, having achieved this standard, you wish to accustom your horse to brief periods of counter-canter (which will suffice for the requirements of the Novice tests and lay the foundations for future schooling), there are two introductory exercises you can do. Remember, however, that the initial purpose of these exercises is to accustom the horse to maintaining counter-canter for very short periods, and the aim is to promote understanding and acceptance, not confusion and resistance.

The first exercise is best performed in an arena larger than standard; indeed, a field with a good, level surface is ideal. Trot, for example, round a suitable field on the right rein then, on a long, straight line, ask quietly and accurately for *left* canter. Once the canter is established, sit very still, quietly maintaining the aids for left canter, especially a little flexion to the left rein. Without changing these aids, or shifting your weight, look a little to the right, open (don't *pull*) the right rein a little, and ask the horse to move in a *gentle* curve to the right. When he responds for a very few strides without resisting or trying to change legs, relax the right rein aid, look ahead, and allow him to straighten. Do not, in the early stages, be too demanding; a very few strides on a slight curve will suffice. Later, as you become more confident of the horse's response, you can ask for a few more strides, or a slightly greater curve (not both at once), but always be ready to straighten the horse before you feel any struggling or resistance. A refinement of this exercise, which you may try at an appropriate stage, is to substitute the straightening up phase with a *very faint* serpentine. Thus, in the example above, after a few strides in a gentle curve to the right (counter-canter), you relax the right rein aid and ride directly into a gentle curve to the left (true canter). As the horse progresses, you can then ask for another gentle curve to the right, back into counter-canter – but never ask for more than you think the horse can give you, either in quantity or degree of the curves.

Once you have achieved a measure of success with this exercise the second, which is pretty much an extension of the first, can be attempted in the school. In, for example, left canter, proceed round the school on the left rein, establishing a good working gait. Use a short side of the school to balance and, if possible, shorten the canter a little, without interfering with the rhythm. As you start down the next long side, just before the first quarter marker, take the horse off the track at a slight angle so that, when level with the B or E marker, he will be no more than a couple of metres from the outside track. As you near the B or E marker, keep the aids for left lead but, as in the previous exercise, ask the horse to curve to the right back to the outside track. Upon reaching the track, cease the aids to move right, and allow the horse to straighten before going through the next corner in correct bend. Once he can do this satisfactorily, you can gradually make the loop a little deeper.

It may be easier, initially, for the horse to show counter-canter when he is travelling in the direction of his convex side (for example, if he is convex left, it may be easier for him to travel left on the right lead rather than vice versa). This is because, in counter-canter, the horse remains flexed in the direction of his leading leg (the right fore, in counter-canter left) and it is easier for the horse to do this when his concave side is to the outside (away from the direction of travel). However, as with all exercises, those in counter-canter must be practised on both reins. Do not get impatient if, at first, the horse does not understand your requirements, or tries to change leg. In the first place, remember that it is natural for the horse to lead in the direction of travel and it is, up to now, what you have always wanted. It is also the horse's natural instinct to maintain his balance, and he will therefore try to change lead if his balance feels threatened – which is a powerful argument in favour of correct rider posture and discreet aids. Furthermore, should you wish, at a later stage, to teach the horse flying changes (when he changes lead on command), you will not have helped your cause if you originally punished him for changing lead when *he* felt it was necessary. Instead, if you experience any problem, canter straight out of the exercise, quietly re-establish trot, and try again, asking only a little at a time.

REIN-BACK

In a good rein-back, the horse steps smoothly straight backwards without resistance. His legs move in diagonal pairs, as in trot, but the tempo is slower. The rider should be able to produce a specific number of steps and then ride straight forwards out of rein-back without any resistance or hesitation.

Performed correctly, rein-back is an exercise in co-ordination of the aids, balance and obedience. It also has a role in developing collection. However, in order to perform the movement (or even learn it) correctly, the horse must already be obedient (submissive in the proper sense) and fairly strong and supple. It is our view that Novice Level is plenty early enough to introduce this movement. This opinion is supported by the practice of various well-known riders, who introduce rein-back at quite a late stage in their training programmes. You should, on no account, attempt to teach it to a horse until he is reasonably supple, accepts the bit and has learnt to go actively forward from your leg. *Half-baked attempts to introduce it roughly, incorrectly or too soon will lay a foundation for serious resistances and evasions.* In the case of horses with skeletally malformed backs, or ongoing weaknesses of the back or hocks, we suggest that this movement be omitted. We also submit that it should not be taught to temperamentally unreliable horses, especially those with a predisposition towards serious napping.

PREPARATION FOR REIN-BACK

1. The horse should never lose the *desire* to go forwards, so you must introduce the movement with tact and patience. The key is the initial recognition by the horse that he is supposed to step backwards – this can be seen almost as an act of faith in the rider, and should be rewarded.

2. Rein-back should always precede (and be followed by) periods of active forward movement; prior to the initial work, the horse must be warmed up, responsive and thinking 'forwards'.

3. Although you want the horse to move backward in a straight line, any tendency towards crookedness in his normal work will be reflected in how he moves backwards. To help keep him as straight as possible, introduce the movement along the arena wall, with the horse positioned so that his concave side is close to the wall.

THE AIDS FOR REIN-BACK

The horse is ridden into a square, attentive halt. There must be a reasonable degree of flexion at the poll and a relaxed jaw; if necessary, a little extra squeezing of the fingers (*not* sawing) into halt can help achieve this. If you get a poor or crooked halt, do not attempt rein-back; try again.

As soon as a good halt is established, rather than easing the aids as usual, use leg pressure as if to ask the horse to move forwards, but do not ease your hands – keep them still and quietly resistant. The horse is then being asked for movement, but is not being allowed to move forwards, so he can only respond by stepping back. As he does so, keep the rein contact but *slightly* reduce the leg pressure, so as not to create tension or make the horse hurry. In retaining the rein contact, it may help to imagine that your hands are holding an invisible wall, which you are drawing back *in accord with* (that is, not faster or slower than) the horse's movement. Keep your seat light to encourage the horse to use his back muscles; this means an easing of weight onto the front of the seat, not standing up or any overt leaning forwards. *Do not* seek to produce backward movement by any backward inclination of your body. On no account should you *pull* back with the reins.

As soon as the desired number of steps have been taken (at first, a couple is sufficient; tests require three or four and

(a)

(b)

(c)

more than six is uncalled for), revert to a full seat, increase your leg pressure and ease your hands at the same time, so that the horse moves immediately forwards. At first, you will have to practice the movement fairly frequently, but do not do so to the extent where the horse starts to anticipate. Interperse your practice by riding normal halts; if the horse shows any tendency to anticipate rein-back, cease practice for the time being and ride plenty of walk/halt/trot transitions. You do not want the horse to offer backward movement of his own accord.

COMMON FAULTS IN REIN-BACK

1. Crookedness. We have seen that this can result from basic lack of straightness in the horse, in which case the long-term cure is to make the horse equally supple on both sides, thus improving all movements. It may be, however, that *you* are sitting crooked or applying the aids unevenly, in which case the cure lies in correcting these faults.

2. Moving backwards above the bit, with stiffened back and short, uneven steps. If the fault is very marked then probably the horse is not physically ready to do the movement, in which case you should wait until he is. Other than this, it may be that your aids are too harsh and uncoordinated; you are using too strong a seat and resisting too strongly with your hands.

• *Correct and incorrect forms of rein-back.*
Correct (top). From a square halt, the horse steps back smoothly and rhythmically.
Incorrect (bottom).
(a) Resistant and above the bit. Rider looks to be pulling back with the reins.
(b) Horse somewhat behind the bit (note incorrect flexion of the neck behind the poll).
(c) Horse is showing obedience in stepping backwards, but he is not stepping correctly in two-time. This may be seen in early attempts and/or in horses who are not quite ready to perform the movement.

3. Dropping behind the bit and hurrying backwards. How serious a fault this is depends upon how marked it is. The mechanics of a horse moving backwards are such that the horse's body starts the backward movement slightly before his legs actually step backwards, so there is a tendency for the legs to try to catch up. This may be exaggerated if you retain too strong a leg pressure and, perhaps, too strong a contact. If you have a mentally quick horse, you may have to keep the aids very light once the movement has started. If you cannot cure the fault by adjusting the aids, it may help to practise rein-back down a *slight slope* on good footing, which may encourage the horse to raise his neck a little. (Patently, this is not advice to encourage him to rush backwards down a steep slope.)

The faults above are very minor compared to a horse running backwards out of control. This is very serious indeed. If a horse learns that he can respond to leg pressure by running backwards, he has discovered a major evasion. Therefore, if you try to teach rein-back and anything of this nature occurs, you must immediately drive the horse vigorously forwards and abandon all further attempts until you are *sure* he has learnt to go forward from your leg. However, to repeat what was said earlier, the most likely cause for such a problem is introducing the movement too soon, or incorrectly and/or to a horse of questionable temperament.

· 10 ·
LINES, CIRCLES, TURNS AND FIGURES

Straight lines, circles and turns are the building blocks upon which all figures are based. It is very easy to take these basic elements for granted and to concentrate on what we perceive to be the more complex aspects of riding but, if attention is not given to the quality of the basic materials, whatever we build with them will be flawed. We should also bear in mind that, in riding, even the most fundamental work can have value, if it is performed correctly.

STRAIGHT LINES

It is easy to think of straight lines as being simply a means of 'getting from A to B', but they are much more important than that. Correct work on straight lines can make some very important contributions to the horse's training:

1. By allowing full, equal action of shoulders and hips on both sides of the horse, it helps to improve the quality of gaits and natural length of stride. Also, by encouraging full forward stretching of the limbs it can help reduce dishing and plaiting, especially if the horse makes either action throughout the length of his forelimbs.

2. By allowing/encouraging full and equal use of the muscles on both sides of the horse, it helps reduce crookedness.

3. Allowing the horse the fullest, easiest use of his limbs encourages impulsion.

4. When a horse is going in a straight line, his spine will be straight from front to back, which is the easiest posture from which to round his back and improve his outline. (The increased impulsion will also help achieve this.)

5. Straight line work will improve the horse's vertical balance and help counter the effects of any leaning in or out on turns, which can be either a cause or effect of stiffness in the leg joints.

Also, riding in a straight line on a light contact at all gaits will provide you with a very good indication of how well you have applied your own skills to the horse's training. Does he keep good balance and rhythm? Does he tend to stretch his head and neck down? Does he go straight?

RIDING STRAIGHT LINES
The first, most obvious, point is that you need to be sure of where you want to go. If *you* haven't made up your mind where you are heading, you can't expect the horse to go straight. (It can help if you fix your eyes on a certain object/arena marker and concentrate upon going straight towards it.)

Second, you must encourage and allow active forward movement. While straight line work will promote this, it is initially easier for the horse to go straight if he is moving forwards energetically.

Third, your own posture and aids should promote, not hinder, correct movement, so you must sit up straight and keep your leg and rein contacts light and even.

Finally, because, as we saw earlier (Chapter 6 – Crookedness) it is quite difficult for any horse to move completely straight, be sensitive to the first slight signs that he is about to go crooked, and correct them as early and lightly as you can by sending him forward and straightening him with your legs, rather than your hands.

COMMON FAULTS IN RIDING STRAIGHT LINES

The common faults which cause loss of straightness involve doing the opposite of the above: being vague about where you are going; not riding forwards (or actually interfering with forward movement); sitting crooked or giving crooked aids; attempting corrections too late and mainly with the reins.

An interesting exercise in straightness and obedience is to ride round the arena a few times trying to keep a set distance (a metre or two) inside the outside track or arena wall. This can be surprisingly difficult and informative! Try on both reins and compare how problems and corrections relate to the horse's 'good' and 'bad' reins. You should, however, do this on the basis of an occasional exercise to check progress, rather than habitually. For a partially trained horse, who is not yet truly 'forward' and substantially straight, it really is quite difficult, and there is the danger that, in trying too hard to succeed, you may end up fiddling about and 'bouncing' the horse between your inside and outside leg, rather like over-steering a car. Therefore, most straight line work should make use of the arena sides, with turns and inclines being ridden from and to distinct markers. Then, when you try this exercise, make a conscious effort not to over-ride the horse and be prepared to accept the result as genuine feedback.

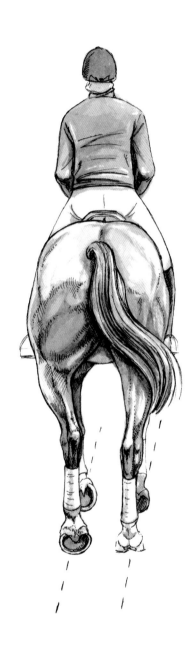

• *Front and rear views of correct work on straight lines.*

CIRCLES

Correct circle work helps improve the horse's suppleness and balance, and engagement of the hind legs. Circles therefore have an important part to play in schooling, but they must be ridden properly; *incorrect* circle work produces none of these advantages, indeed, it simply provokes evasions which are more likely to have the opposite effect. As with all exercises, the aim is to get the horse working correctly on large circles, and then gradually reduce the size. Asking too soon for circles which are smaller than the horse can readily perform is a prime cause of evasions and loss of activity.

PREPARATION FOR A CIRCLE

Moving on a circle is physically harder for a horse than moving on a straight line. Therefore, before you start a circle, the horse must be moving in a good, active rhythmic gait.

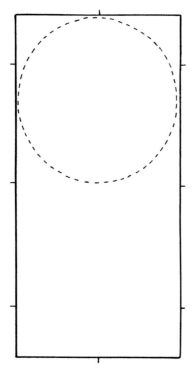

• *Correct location of a 20 m circle from A or C. Note that this does not entail going through the corners of the arena, as if going large.*

Although the collecting effect of the circle may help to improve the *quality* of the gait, this can only happen if there is activity to start with, and if activity and rhythm are retained. For this reason, when riding circles, you should always think 'forward and round'. This does not mean that the 'round' is less important (it is the very essence of a circle), but it is much more likely to happen if the 'forward' element remains in place.

The second point about preparation is that you must have a very clear picture in your mind of the size and location of the circle you intend to ride. Imagine it painted on the ground and aim to start it smoothly, at the right place. If it doesn't begin in the right place, it can't finish there *and be round*. (Further to this, if you are going to ride dressage tests, examine all the circle work involved and *check precisely* what is required. Many riders throw away marks in tests by simply not knowing or caring about the circle work. A prime example of this is a 20 m circle from A or C *which cannot possibly* entail going through the corners of the arena.)

RIDING A CIRCLE

As mentioned, the fundamental point is to start it in the right place. A second point to consider is that the first segment (the first two or three strides) is the most crucial. If the circle is started correctly, with activity and the right amount of bend, all you have to do is keep what you've got, and you will get back to the starting point. However, if things go wrong at this early stage, the whole exercise may become a process of adjustment, correction and 'looking for' the figure.

Before considering the specific aids, we should mention the importance of sitting upright, in a good posture, throughout the circle. Any leaning in or out will simply unbalance the horse and disturb the figure.

To begin the circle, your inside hand flexes the inside rein a little to guide the horse onto the circle. With virtually untrained or very stiff horses, this aid may entail opening the rein a little (moving the hand a couple of inches sideways *and slightly forwards*), but it MUST NEVER entail pulling backwards. With horses who have even a modicum of training, provided there is an acceptable rein contact, this aid need be no more than a

● *Bending correctly on a circle.*

subtle request to look on the right direction.[1] While this is the aid that literally leads the horse onto the circle, it never operates in isolation. The legs act jointly to mould the whole of the horse's body into the required shape. Your inside leg, on the girth, acts as a point of reference for the horse – a sort of inside rail that says 'you must keep outside this'. Your outside leg, behind the girth, keeps the horse's quarters tracking correctly, preventing them from swinging to the outside. Your legs also act as necessary to maintain the required degree of activity. Although it does not act in isolation, it is the inside leg that plays the major role on a circle – by keeping the horse's inside hind leg active, it also helps to sustain his balance. This is especially noticeable if you canter a somewhat unbalanced horse on a circle: you will find that firm, supportive aids from your inside leg (backed up by a quieter outside leg kept on the horse) will greatly assist the horse to retain his balance and stay in the required gait.[2] The outside rein plays a crucial but subtle role in the moulding of the horse. It is important, both in terms of keeping the horse on the aids and on the circle, that contact is maintained in the outside rein, but the important word here is 'maintained'. As we shall see shortly, it is a fundamental error to try to hold the horse on the circle by pulling on the outside rein. However, it can also be the case that riders who misinterpret the concept of inside leg into outside hand[3] can simply keep too strong a contact with the outside rein, which interferes with the horse's ability to flex his neck in accord with the shape of the circle. And this is the crux of the matter. When a horse is circling, because there is width to his body, his outer side has to stretch more than his inner side. (This is simple geometry: the outside – the tread – of a tyre has a larger circumference than the inner aspect that meets the wheel.) Since a rider starts out on a circle with both reins of even length, the outside hand has to give forward on the circle to accommodate the outside stretching of the horse. This is where the subtlety comes in, because it is still necessary to retain the contact. If this is lost, then control of the horse's forehand is lost. Thus the appropriate action of the outside rein depends on conscious, two-way communication between horse and rider. The rider cannot rely upon some arbitrary positioning

[1] As an exercise in checking what is required, stand behind a friend and rest your hands, palms inward, on their cheeks. Feel how little movement of your hands is required to turn their head in a required direction. Remember that, when riding a horse on a circle, you do not want any more flexion in the head and neck than is required in the rest of the body.
[2] If it is to play this role, the inside leg must not be drawn up or flap; it must remain at its full length against the horse's side, with weight in the heel. To help achieve this leg position (in any context) without leaning or forcing an artificial (fixed) flexion of the ankle, try imagining that your legs are made of hot lead, which is melting down into your boots.
[3] This, briefly, describes the energy, generated primarily by the rider's inside leg, 'filling' (travelling into) the outside rein. Simply putting the inside leg on firmly, and taking a firm contact with the outside rein, does not fulfil these criteria.

of the outside hand, but must listen to the sensations being communicated by the horse, and apply feel.

As mentioned earlier, the smaller the circle, the harder it is for the horse to perform well, and the more crucial it becomes to sit well and apply the aid accurately.

COMMON FAULTS IN RIDING CIRCLES

1. Loss of activity. As mentioned, active forward movement is a major factor in good circle work. Loss of activity suggests either lack of preparation or inattention on the rider's part, or that the horse is being asked to perform circles that are too small for his stage of training.

2. Wrong shape. This either signifies lack of forethought by the rider, or is a consequence of evasions by the horse uncorrected, or caused by, the rider's aids (see below).

3. Trying to pull the horse round with the inside rein. This will block the action of the horse's inner side, interfere with his forward movement, and make him swing his quarters out. If he is reluctant to bend onto the circle, use stronger leg aids, especially a stronger holding pressure with the inside leg (not an on-off action). Remember, most horses will bend more readily in one direction than the other (see Chapter 6 Stiffness and Crookedness).

• *Incorrect circling: rider pulls back with the inside rein, constricting movement of the horse's inside lateral and causing the hindquarters to swing out sideways.*

• *Incorrect circling: rider tries to hold horse out on the circle with the outside rein, causing wrong bend and incorrect tracking.*

4. Trying to hold the horse out on the circle by hanging onto the outside rein. A horse may try to make a circle smaller, or 'fall in' if he is anticipating the turn (for example towards companions, or a jump), or when he is circling to his 'soft' (concave) side. In the first case, he is trying to fall round the circle on his shoulders. If you hang onto the outside rein, he will just lean on your hand and swing his quarters in. The shape of the circle will be lost. In an extreme case (an excitable, badly schooled horse jumping) he may end up going sideways. A horse who tries to cut in like this must be kept out on the circle by your inside leg. If the horse has been badly schooled in the past, this will be difficult to do at first, but it is important to persist because this is the only way to remedy the fault.

The horse who tries to fall in when circling to his concave side is an example of the fact that crookedness is a two-sided problem. This matter has been discussed in Chapter 6 Crookedness – circle work.

When addressing faults on circles, remember that it is impossible to correct them by relying solely on the rein aids. You have to put the whole horse on the circle – not just his forehand.

STANDARD TURNS IN MOTION

A standard 90 degree turn (for example, through a corner or across the arena) is ridden as a quarter of a circle. This means that all of the criteria applicable to riding a circle must also be applied to a turn. Furthermore, if we accept that the first segment of a circle is the most crucial, we should be mindful that a 90 degree turn constitutes *almost all* of that segment. It is easy to see, then, that preparation is a highly important element in riding turns.

Since turns are usually based upon rather small circles (of which more in a moment), it is very important that the horse begins a turn not only with a good degree of activity, but also in good balance. A properly executed half-halt (improving the balance, whilst retaining the forward impulse) is therefore a valuable part of the preparation. The other aspect of preparation relates to knowing where the turn is going to begin. If you

intend to ride a turn that is a quarter of a 10 m circle, this figure will have a radius of 5 m, which means that the turn must begin 5 m from the line you intend to finish on. For example, if you intend to turn in this manner across the arena from E to B, you will have to begin the turn 5 m before E, otherwise you will overshoot the turn. Understanding this will help you to avoid making late, abrupt turns, of the type that involve urgent tugging on the inside rein. As we have seen, this is a major error in riding circles. If committed on a turn – especially a tight turn – it will destroy the activity of the gait and seriously unbalance the horse. (Indeed, if you do it at canter on slippery going, you may even pull the horse over.)

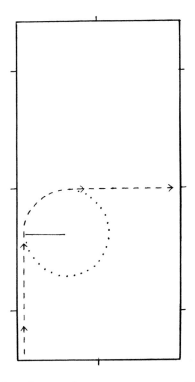

• *Diagram showing the need to prepare properly for a turn across the arena. This turn is based on a quarter of a 10 m circle – the sort of turn you may need to make in trot on a novice horse. As the horse's training and balance improve, it will be possible to base turns on smaller circles, but it will always be necessary to begin the turn before the relevant marker is reached.*

(a)   (b)

• *Turning is an example of communicating through the aids. Rider (a) is using a substantially open rein (which might be necessary when turning a young or unschooled horse), but his posture shows that the aids are being coordinated to channel the horse through the turn. Rider (b) is simply pulling back on the inside rein; the pony's neck is substantially overbent to the exclusion of his body, and his steps have shortened. He will slew round the corner with loss of correct bend and activity.*

This brings us to consider the size of circle upon which turns should be based. Logically, this will be influenced by the gait in which the turn is made, and the individual horse's stage of training. According to the competition rules, turns in dressage tests in the working gaits should be ridden as a quarter of a 6 m circle. However, it is fair to say that very few partly trained horses, ridden by relatively inexperienced riders, are capable of performing such a turn smoothly, without incorrect bend or loss of rhythm. This applies in particular to canter, but may also be true of trot. The basis of the turn (the 6 m circle) is simply too small for such combinations. Certainly, in general schooling at home, you should ride turns of a size that the horse can manage fairly readily, without loss of activity or balance. These turns can be made gradually tighter, in line with work that improves the horse's suppleness and balance, but they should not be made tight on an arbitrary basis, just for the sake of it. So far as tests are concerned, it remains sensible to ride your turns on the basis of what the horse can do at home (your judgement may be supplemented by practice runs of figures in a particular test). Although there is a considerable accent on accuracy in dressage tests, this is one instance where an intelligent trade off can pay dividends, the rationale being that slightly bigger turns, in which balance and rhythm are maintained, will score higher than tighter turns, poorly performed, in which these qualities are lost. (Further to this, it is important to remember that movements in tests are not performed in isolation – they flow into other movements. Thus, if important qualities are lost in one movement, this may well have repercussions on the next.) However, we would emphasise that, if this compromise is made, there can be no excuse for inaccuracy – riding somewhat wide turns and still missing the intended line will not impress the judge. The prime example of this is turning onto the centre line in trot, a movement that occurs towards the end of virtually all basic level tests. Strictly speaking, this should be ridden from the long side as follows: a quarter of a 6 m circle; 4 m straight; a quarter of a 6 m circle. In practice, many novice combinations do well to show any intermediate straightness at all. However, if you decide to ride this figure as a continuous turn from the long side (that is, half a 10 m circle), it is imperative that this flows smoothly and accurately *onto* the centre line. It may concentrate the mind if you remember that the judge is ideally positioned to see any discrepancy in

this movement. Similar comments apply to the mirror image of this turn; that *from* the centre line. However, especially indoors, because the long side is more tangible than the centre line, this turn is somewhat easier to ride.

OTHER WAYS OF TURNING

Apart from turns performed as quarter circles there are three other ways in which a horse can turn, which we can consider briefly.

Turn on the forehand. The horse turns in a pivot around the foreleg to the 'inside' of the direction of the turn (if his head turns to the left, the pivoting is around the left foreleg). This turn is useful for dealing with gates when riding out, as a means of teaching the horse to obey the lateral leg aids and as an exercise in coordination of aids by the rider. However, since it is ridden from the halt, it has no practical application for turning in motion.

To perform a turn on the forehand, the horse is ridden forward into halt (on an inside track a couple of metres from the wall, if in an arena). As soon as the halt is established, the rider asks for a *very slight* flexion of the horse's head in the direction to which it is to turn. The rider's leg on the same side then slides back a little behind the girth, and pushes the hindquarters sideways, in the opposite direction from which the head is to turn. While the rider's motivating leg should remain on the horse, it should push in a pulsating way, in time with the horse's steps. If it simply 'shoves', this may cause the horse to skid round in a hurried, unbalanced way. The rein contact should remain constant, to prevent any stepping forward, but if the horse does step forward slightly, the rider should not react with a harsh tug of the reins, because this will cause the horse to hollow and step backwards – a much worse fault. If the horse does attempt to step backwards, a mild attempt can be corrected by the rider's outside leg, on the girth. If the attempt to step backwards is more marked, the sideways pushing of the inside leg should be interrupted, and both legs used to correct it – if necessary, riding briskly forwards out of the

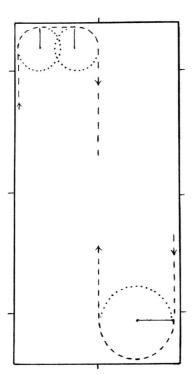

● *Two ways of turning down the centre line: (a) strictly correct; (b) half a 10 m circle from the long side.*

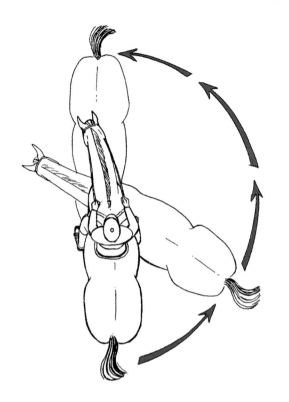

movement. Even good, correct turns should be followed immediately by active forward movement.

Although, in principle, the horse can be turned through 360 degrees, in practise, most turns need be through only 90 degrees, and this is certainly enough for early attempts. Two other points to note: first, as with all work, the horse will probably turn more readily in one direction than the other and second, practising the movement should be done occasionally, liberally interspersed with normal halts, otherwise a keen, intelligent horse will start to anticipate a turn and fidget on every halt (as if asking 'Which way do you want my bum to go?').

• *The turn on the forehand. Diagram shows a half-turn on the forehand to the left (i.e. the horse's head turns towards the left). The picture sequence shows the same movement. Note that, in an arena, it is necessary to begin the turn a couple of metres in from the outside track, in order that the horse has room to make the turn.*

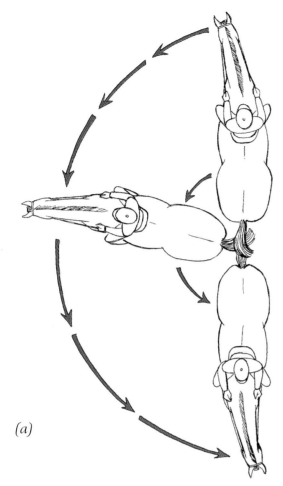

(a)

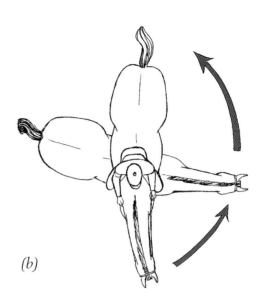

(b)

• *In the turn on the haunches (a) the horse pivots around his inside hind leg, which itself describes a small circle. This turn is the basis of pirouette work. In the turn on the centre (b) the horse swivels around his own centre. Although it can be ridden under saddle, this turn has limited applications.*

Turn on the haunches. This, ridden in walk, is the foundation of pirouette work (canter pirouette being one of the most advanced movements in dressage). Essentially, the horse pivots around the inside hind leg, which remains stepping in sequence with the gait (that is, it is not planted on the ground). Initially, however, this turn is introduced in such a way that it is incorporated into continued forward movement: the horse turns in motion, but the hind legs describe a smaller circle than the forelegs. Performed correctly, turns on the haunches engage and strengthen the hindquarters and lighten the forehand. However, although the turn requires an interplay of all the aids, there is an inherent risk that the rider will be tempted simply to pull the horse round with

the inside rein. If this is wrong on normal turns of larger diameter, it is disastrous in turns on the haunches. Therefore, this work should not be attempted until horse/rider combinations have established a good rapport in normal turns in motion, and can perform these fluently, maintaining balance, bend and rhythm. Furthermore, since this work really requires some degree of collection in the walk, it can be considered as something for the future.

Turn on the centre. In this turn, the horse's forehand turns in one direction, while his hindquarters step the other way, so that he swivels literally round his own centre. (Holding a pencil at its centre and rotating your wrist in one direction will give you the idea). This is a turn that horses will sometimes carry out naturally when manoeuvring in a confined space but, even ridden correctly, it has limited value under saddle, and can only be ridden out of walk. It is notable, however, that incorrect travesties of this turn are often performed by horses whose riders make too much use of the inside rein, and neither hold the horse out and keep him going forward with the inside leg, not control the quarters with the outside leg. As we said earlier, turns of this nature – especially at the faster gaits – will destroy rhythm, activity and balance.

BASIC FIGURES

The figures used in basic schooling and required in lower level tests are made up of parts of circles and straight lines. Therefore, if you ride them applying the principles which will produce correct circles and straight lines, you should produce good figures.

When schooling at home you can (and should) use whatever figures suit your purpose; the only rule is that the horse should be capable of performing them correctly. If you are preparing for a test, however, it is important that you understand precisely how and where the required figures fit into the arena and that you spend some time practising them. No matter how well you ride a figure in a test, you will lose marks if it is the wrong size, or in the wrong place.

To avoid clutter, movements are described in very brief terms on test sheets, and the descriptions make certain assumptions of the rider's understanding. Interpreting them should not be too difficult, because the figures are described in geometrical terms and have to fit into an arena of a defined size and shape. Therefore, a little thought should make things clear. However, not everyone is good at geometry so, if you are in *any doubt at all* about any instruction, the first thing to do is check it. The British Dressage rule book has a section Notes on the Interpretation of Dressage Test Sheets which may help, or you can ask a judge, instructor or experienced competitor. Further advice about preparing for a dressage test is given in the next chapter.

Figures in common use are described below. Remarks about riding these figures in a test – especially those referring to accuracy – should be considered equally pertinent to schooling at home.

INCLINES

An incline is a turn at an angle of less than ninety degrees, for example, a turn across a diagonal. When riding an incline from a straight line you must, as with turns, think ahead and prepare to guide the horse correctly onto the new line of travel at the appropriate marker. Do not run the risk of finding yourself almost past the marker, trying to tug the horse into a late, crooked change of direction.

In some tests, there is a requirement to ride a half-circle from the outside track, followed by an incline back to the track. In this case, you should have a very mental picture of the whole figure and should ride the incline by coming smoothly off the half-circle at the appropriate tangent point. The most common directional error in this movement is coming off what was supposed to be a half-circle too late. If you intend to return to the track at a set marker, you will then have to ride a somewhat curved line (curved away from the direction of the half-circle) rather than an incline, to reach the marker. If the test allows you to return to the track between markers, you will do so at an undesirably steep angle.

At the end of an incline, you should rejoin the outside track smoothly, retaining a constant rhythm.

LOOPS

Loops are exercises in the coordination of directional aids. On a test sheet, a loop is defined by its points of departure from and return to the track, and by its greatest distance from the track (which will be at its mid-point). For example, a loop between K and H 5 m from the track requires you to be 5 m from the track when you pass E (halfway between K and H). To ride such a loop, as you reach the K marker, direct the horse off the track as if you were about to begin an incline across the arena but, as you leave the track, ask for a little left bend. You must be looking towards the centre point of loop, asking for the amount of bend which will take you smoothly through it. Maintain this bend until you near the H marker, then gently reverse your directional aids, asking for a little right bend, so that you return smoothly to the outside track. Take care that you ride the last part of the figure correctly; do not finish it by using your inside leg to push the horse's hindquarters sideways onto the track, because this is not what is required.

SERPENTINES

A serpentine is a series of equal sized loops curving in alternate directions. Each serpentine is defined by the number of loops it contains and the area it covers. Depending upon its definition, a serpentine may or may not have straight lines between the curves; if it does, it will be easier to ride, because the straight lines give you more time to change the horse's bend.

An example of what is, in effect, a two-loop serpentine is the figure of two 10 m half-circles BXE to change the rein. This figure causes problems for many riders because they attempt a sudden, major change of bend at X, which makes the second part of the figure go awry. The secret of riding this movement is to ensure a good, accurate first half-circle, then to ride the horse straight for one stride through X, before commencing the second half-circle. This figure acknowledges the reality of equine physiology (you are riding a horse, not a snake) and allows time for the change of bend. In a test, you must not overdo the straight section but, if you ride accurately, the straight stride will

• *Some basic school figures. (a) Half-circle followed by an incline back to the track. (b) 5 m loop between quarter markers. (c) A very basic serpentine – two 10 m half-circles through X to change the rein. (d) A three-loop serpentine to cover the whole arena – note that loops should be equal in size and shape.*

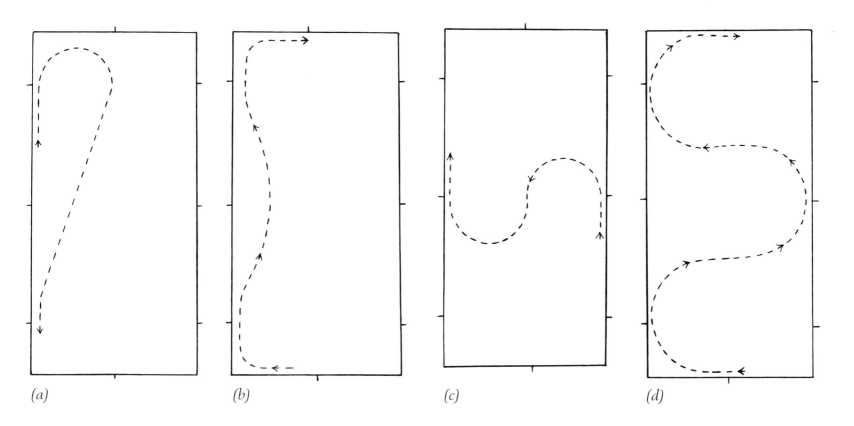

(a)   (b)   (c)   (d)

appear simply as the ending of the first half-circle and the beginning of the second. You should apply the same principle to any serpentine where the curves appear to follow each other immediately and, in any serpentine which has obvious straight sections, make good use of these sections to straighten the horse and prepare him for the next loop.

The most common fault with all serpentines is that they are ridden inaccurately, with uneven loops. They are a prime example of figures where a proper understanding of layout and proper preparation are required. You should note especially that, once one loop has been ridden inaccurately, this is *bound* to affect the rest of the figure.

It is, therefore, a good idea to practise serpentines at home. Indeed, trotting three- and four-loop serpentines to cover the whole arena is a good exercise for both horse and rider. It will improve your aid applications and the horse's attentiveness and lateral suppleness on both sides, as well as giving you a greater feel for the space in the arena and how to use it.

·11·
RIDING DRESSAGE TESTS

Although this book has repeatedly made the point that dressage is training, there is one major difference between training at home and riding a dressage test.

While a wise rider will be seeking to produce overall improvement in the horse, a good proportion of work at home will concentrate upon some particular aspect of training: improving suppleness, introducing new ideas and so on. With much of this work, a sensible rider will take time to set things up as favourably as possible, to give the best possible chance of achieving the key aim. For example, a rider who is working on improving transitions to canter will not start asking for them until satisfied with the quality of the trot. Indeed, even when such a rider has decided to canter at the next marker, if the quality of trot is lost for some reason, the intended transition will be abandoned until the trot is restored. The aim is not to get some sort of transition, but an *improved* transition, and this will not be achieved out of a poor basic gait. The same principle will apply in many circumstances when training at home.

In order to conform to the requirements of a dressage test, however, the rider does not have such options, but is obliged to perform a prescribed series of movements at pre-determined times and places. This reinforces the view that, although we quite legitimately use individual exercises and movements during the training process, the ultimate aim of training is not to teach the horse to perform certain movements in isolation, but to have him consistently on the aids – mentally and physically able and willing to respond to any of our requirements at any time. Thus, a dressage test is really a test to discover to what extent a horse is on the aids; the movements required merely represent examples of the type of work he should be able to perform at a given level of training.

There is a lesson to be learnt from this, which is especially important for anyone wanting to compete, but also a useful check on overall training. When schooling at home, it is good practice sometimes to concentrate exclusively upon the horse's responsiveness – the extent to which he is on the aids. A good way of doing this, depending on the horse's level of training, is to get the best working trot you can achieve (but do wait until you get it) and play with it; moving around the arena and deciding, almost on the spur of the moment, what to ask for next. If the gait is good, and the horse listening, you should be able to ask for halt, or canter, or a little lengthening, or a small circle, or leg-yielding – whatever takes your fancy – and get a good response to your request. If you feel confident that you can do this, you can be pretty sure that your horse is on the aids; if, however, there is an element of doubt, then he is probably not quite there. The one thing to beware of with this exercise is that you do not make your decisions about what to ask for (or give the aids) too abruptly. However, if your horse really is on the aids, then you probably won't feel the need to.

RULES AND REGULATIONS FOR TESTS

Virtually all Preliminary and Novice Level dressage competitions in Britain are run under the rules of British Dressage, British Eventing or the Pony Club. (The Riding Clubs Committee follow

British Dressage or British Eventing rules, as appropriate.[1])

Although the rules of these bodies are broadly similar, there are some minor, but highly significant, variations. While it is not the purpose of this book to analyse these differences in detail, all competitors are strongly advised to check which rules apply to any particular test and, if possible, to obtain a current copy of the relevant rule book (these are updated annually).

Particular attention should be paid to the sections relating to rider's dress and equipment, permitted tack both for riding-in and during the test, and the performance of the test itself.

The single most useful rule book for anyone riding tests under various rules is that of British Dressage,[2] because it contains a summary list of main items of tack and equipment permitted or forbidden under its own and other rules. This is not, how-ever, a *complete* analysis of all points so, if in doubt, check with the show secretary, ring steward or judge. Do not run the risk of riding a good test and being eliminated for infringing a rule you were unaware of!

PREPARING FOR A TEST

Different people have different temperaments and different ways of learning. Horses also differ, both in temperament and in strengths, weaknesses and overall levels of training. Because of these differences, it is not possible to say that there is one correct way of preparing for and riding a dressage test. However, there are some guidelines which should be useful in most circumstances, so let us have a look at them.

UNDERSTANDING THE REQUIREMENTS

In order to ride a test as well as possible, you must first understand fully what is required. As mentioned in the previous chapter, this means that you must have a thorough knowledge of the layout of an arena, and of how the different figures required in the test fit into it. Since the layout of the short (40 m x 20 m) arena is less complex than that of the 60 m x 20 m arena, the individual movements and tests performed in it also tend to be less complex. Therefore, it makes sense to choose a short arena test for your first few ventures into competition.

[1] Readers outside Britain should refer to their equivalent organisations – see note in Preface.
[2] Or the equivalent national body.

THE NEED TO MEMORISE THE TEST

Under most sets of rules (although not when the test is part of a horse trial) it is permissible to have the test commanded (the movements called out by an assistant). If a *suitable* commander is available, this can be useful for an experienced competitor who is riding several different tests in one day, or competing at short notice. It is, however, something that the less experienced competitor is advised to avoid – however tempting it may seem at first sight.

The first reason for this is that commanding a test well is harder than it might seem. To be of any help, a commander must have a good experience of dressage movements (and preferably the specific test), a good sense of timing, good voice projection and a knowledge of the rules (if a commander starts giving advice, the competitor will be eliminated). If these qualities are lacking, the result is likely to be a shambles.

The second reason for avoiding having tests commanded is that, in many cases, this is simply a way of ducking the issue of learning the test properly – which is much the best way to proceed if you want a good result.

That said, it is a fact that many inexperienced competitors worry about their ability to learn the test, and about what will happen if they make a mistake. To deal with the second point first, the judge will signal to stop a competitor who has gone wrong, tell them the nature of the error and, usually, try to ensure that they are clear about how to continue. There is a two-point penalty for a first error of course, four points for a second and eight for a third (these penalties being cumulative). In practice, however, it is fairly rare for a competitor to go wrong more than once. This is because, in most cases, riders do not really forget the test – they simply suffer a moment's aberration and realise what they have done wrong almost as soon as they've done it.

Nevertheless, no one *likes* to go wrong and, in fact, being a little concerned that you *might* will help to make you more thorough in learning the test! This is a good thing because the more thoroughly you know it, the better. If you can commit it to memory to the extent where your recall becomes automatic, you will be free to expend all your mental energies on riding the horse as well as possible, rather than on wondering what to do next.

COMMITTING THE TEST TO MEMORY

When you first start competing, it makes sense to attempt just one test per competition, so that you can give your full attention to learning and riding it as well as possible. Also, it is a good idea to give yourself plenty of time to learn it without rushing. With experience and a background knowledge of the popular tests you will, if necessary, be able to learn a basic test adequately in a very short time. However, this is never really desirable and attempting it in the early stages will probably result in panic and confusion. Ideally, therefore, you should start to learn your first test several days before the competition, spending a few quiet minutes at a time on it.

The first point to consider is that a test is divided into numbered movements mainly for ease of judging and marking. From a rider's point of view, there is no great need to memorise where each numbered movement starts; indeed, rather than thinking of it as a series of individual parts, it is better to think of the test as a smoothly flowing whole, because this is how you will be aiming to ride it.

Read through the test a few times, concentrating on getting a clear mental picture of the sequence and route, the gaits performed and the location of transitions – especially whether they are to be performed at a marker, or between markers. Do not, however, make a conscious effort to try to remember the whole test in one go; instead, just let it start to sink in.

How you consolidate the learning process is up to you; everyone has a preferred method. Some people sketch out an arena plan and practise running through the test with a pencil, using different lines for different gaits. Others use ready made crib sheets bought from equestrian bookshops – others 'walk, trot and canter' round the garden, or hop toy horses round the dining room table! Exactly *how* you learn is unimportant; what is important is that, if you even *think* that you've gone wrong, you should immediately refer back to the test sheet. You do not want to make a wrong guess and have an error of course engraved on your memory.

Once you have reached the stage at which you can run through the test without error, it is useful to visualise actually riding it. Imagine that you are in the arena riding the movements to a realistic timescale on your own horse, at his current stage of training (if you do this properly, it will take about five minutes

to imagine the whole test). This exercise will help really imprint the test on your memory, and it will make you more aware of the places where you will have to prepare for the more demanding figures and movements.

CHECKING YOUR PRACTICE ARENA

Assuming you get the chance, it obviously makes sense to practise riding the test. However, such practice can prove misleading if it is carried out in an arena that is not of the appropriate size or correct proportions.

An increasing number of Preliminary and Novice Level tests are now designed for the 60 m x 20 m arena.[3] These, patently, cannot be practised in a 40 m x 20 m arena. However, it is possible to practise short arena tests in a 60 m x 20 m arena. The drawback is that this will give you a false impression of available space, which may come back to haunt you during the test itself. For example, the long diagonal of the 60 m x 20 m arena is about 50 per cent longer than that of the short arena; the 'long side' distance between the quarter markers (e.g. HK) is 48 m in the long arena, as opposed to 28 m in the short arena. The different dimensions also have enormous effects on figures such as the three-loop serpentine and, in the long arena, a 20 m circle from A or C will not go anywhere near X. Therefore, if you have no choice but to practise a short arena test in a long arena, you should concentrate mainly on rehearsing the *sequence* of the movements, and be very mindful of the fact that, in the actual test, you will have substantially less time and room.

An even more insidious problem can arise if you are compelled to practise in an arena which is of neither standard size nor proportions. Although the majority of yards nowadays have an arena which is of one standard size or the other, some do not. Such yards may have an arena in which the marker letters are positioned in correct *sequence* around the perimeter, but the arena itself may not only be non-standard in size; it may also have different *proportions* from a standard arena. Practising in such an arena can be very misleading for an inexperienced competitor. Indeed, if it is significantly smaller than a standard arena *and* of incorrect proportions, the process will prove so difficult and

---

[3] Practices may vary in other countries.

misleading that it is best not attempted. If it is significantly bigger, in some respect, than the test arena, then problems may arise similar to those experienced when practising a 20 m x 40 m test in a 20 m x 60 m arena. Indeed, one could say that a 20 m x 60 m arena is a 20 m x 40 m arena out of proportion – but at least they have the same width! If, however, a completely non-standard practice arena is, say, 30 m wide, then a genuine 15 m half-circle will put you on the centre line (rather than the three-quarter line), while a presumed '15 m half-circle' which puts you on the three-quarter line of that arena will actually be a 22.5 m half-circle (i.e. bigger than the entire width of a standard arena).

If you have such an arena at your home yard it is sensible to mark out an area of approximately standard size, preferably with cones. You may also have to ignore or cover up existing marker letters which are in the wrong place (e.g. 'quarter markers' placed in corners), or perhaps make your own temporary ones, but the more realistic feel your temporary arena gives you will make it worth the effort.

MOUNTED PRACTICE

When you practise the test mounted, the first aim should be to improve your familiarity with it. Therefore, do not start to practise it until you are pretty sure that you will be able to complete it without any error of course. In case you do go wrong, have a copy of the test available, either in your pocket or in the hands of a helpful friend. Once you have warmed up, run straight through the test. If any movement is performed poorly, do not interrupt the test for a schooling session; you can return to the problem afterwards to consider whether it was just a lapse, or whether the movement represents a weak area in the horse's training which requires more attention before the competition.

One or two runs-through should satisfy you that you know the test, and may also make you more aware of figures or transitions which require special care. At this stage, rather than just running through the test, you can start thinking in terms of presenting it well. However, be sparing in the number of times you practise the whole test; it is no good if you become bored or careless, or your horse gets stale or starts anticipating. Also, practise the test only on those occasions when you would normally do flatwork; do not neglect your other activities

(jumping, hacking etc.), because these provide a welcome variety for you and your horse.

As a guide, your flatwork in the days before the test can proceed along these lines: ride the horse in, run through the test, then proceed with your normal schooling programme, paying a little extra attention to any test movement which is causing difficulty. Run through the test once more, then wind down on a long rein.

RIDING-IN

The purpose of riding-in before a competition is to make the horse as active, supple and responsive as possible, so that he goes into the arena in a condition to perform to the best of his ability.

Different horses need different amounts of riding-in, and experience may show that a certain individual's needs will vary in different circumstances. However, each horse tends to have an average time which can be used as a guideline, and you should ensure that you always allow yourself at least this average, whatever it may be. If you are taking a horse to a competition for the first time, the sensible approach is to allow yourself the amount of time it usually takes to achieve his best work at home and, if he is inexperienced or a nervous type, add an extra twenty minutes or so for hacking him quietly round the showground to settle him before you start trying to ride-in.

Remember, the time allotted for riding-in should be used for that purpose – allow *extra* time for unboxing, tacking up, collecting your number and queuing for hot dogs.

Different venues have different amounts of space available for riding-in. If you have any choice in the matter, go to shows where the amount of space available is generous. Give yourself, and other competitors as much room as possible, so you can concentrate on the job in hand, rather than avoiding head-on collisions.

When you start riding-in, do so in the same way as you would at home. Give the horse a chance to warm up and wake up before you make any serious demands. Once he is ready to start working properly, be aware of what you are trying to achieve; use your knowledge of the horse and the schooling movements to work him gradually towards a peak. To improve activity, trot (and later, canter) straight lines and large circles. If the horse is nervous or excitable, start off on large circles in rising trot on a light contact, keeping calm yourself and using *your* rhythm to influence the horse, then concentrate upon simple figures in walk and trot until he is calm and attentive. Once the horse is both physically active and mentally calm, figure work (smaller circles and serpentines) will help improve suppleness. Transitions will help improve responsiveness, activity and balance, if they are ridden correctly with the emphasis on the horse going *forwards*.

Whilst riding-in, be careful not to let bad mental attitudes interfere with your progress. On the one hand, do not be careless in your riding of movements which the horse usually performs well. If you are careless, he probably won't do as well as you'd expected, and this will make you disappointed or irritated, when a more positive approach on your part would have produced good work and increased your confidence. On the other hand, be careful about how you approach the horse's weak movements. There is no point in adopting a defeatist attitude and just going through the motions, because this is almost certain to produce the worst possible result and confirm your fears. On the other hand, an aggressive last-minute effort to wring some major improvement from the horse will also be unhelpful; it will probably just upset him and set up resistances. Instead, be realistic – try for the best response you can reasonably expect, and be content with that.

Finally, however the riding-in period has gone, spend the last few minutes doing whatever work the horse is most likely to perform willingly and well so that, when you enter the test arena, you have a happy and cooperative partner.

RIDING THE TEST

At the moment you enter the arena, you and the horse both have a certain degree of ability. The test lasts for about five minutes – not long enough for either of you to improve dramatically – so it is pretty certain that you will not do *better* in the test than you have been doing in your recent work. Therefore, you can either do your best, or something less than your best. The main influences which will determine how you perform will be your attitude and your judgement. These will either *allow* you and your horse to do your best, or else detract from your joint performance.

In practice, few competitors ride to the very best of their ability in a test, and few horses produce their best performance. This is largely cause and effect. Sometimes, it is the rider who affects the horse; at other times, the horse becoming nervous or uncooperative in the arena can provoke errors in the rider.

The fact that minor problems and errors invade most tests is not surprising. Most competitors naturally experience a degree of nervous tension; there is the pressure of trying to get everything right first time, and most people are trying to disguise some weakness in the horse's training – which can lead to errors of judgement and technique. To pretend that such things do not happen is pointless; it is far better to recognise that they *do* and consider how to minimise their effects.

First, it is a good idea, as you make your way towards the arena, to have one more swift mental run-through of the test. Then, if your mind goes blank in the moments before you start the test (as happens with a lot of people), you can reassure yourself that you *do* know it, which should help prevent you from starting the test in a state of panic and concentrating solely on where to go.

Your attitude to the test may well be influenced by *why* you are doing it. If it is a first attempt for you and/or your horse, it is all too easy to be negative: 'I don't know why I'm doing this', 'I just want to get it over' and so on. In such circumstances, you can easily find yourself riding an almost apologetic test, as if you were saying to the judge 'I'm sorry about this – I'll be out of your way in a minute'. This approach will just result in a hurried, careless test which will confirm your worst fears. Therefore, instead of thinking of the judge as an examiner it can be helpful to think more in terms of a visiting instructor – someone whose comments you welcome. Then, rather than 'apologising' for your test, you will be more inclined to 'present' it saying, in effect, 'This is the work we're doing at the moment, please give me your opinion'.

Negative attitudes can also arise if you find yourself in more advanced company, especially if you find yourself following a very proficient partnership. The point to remember here is one that we touched upon in the Introduction – in competitive dressage, the competition is mainly against yourself. Unlike most other sports, you have no influence whatsoever over your fellow competitors; if they have better, more experienced horses than you, or simply ride better, or both, they are going to get better scores. Therefore, there is little point in trying to beat them or even (except insofar as you may learn something), comparing yourself to them. Instead, your aim is to beat your own previous performance;

every time you make progress, you are winning. In your first test, this may be a matter of conquering pre-test nerves and completing the test without error; in the next, it may be getting 6 for a movement for which you previously achieved 4. The point is, if you can adopt this sort of attitude, you have something positive to aim for, and are less likely to be overawed by other competitors whose circumstances differ from your own.

Another situation which can produce a lot of pressure is riding for a team; no one wants to let their team mates down. However, if you have been picked for a Riding Club team, the probability is that you have had a reasonable amount of experience or, if it is a novice team, at least similar experience to the others. What you should bear in mind is that all horse sports are notoriously unpredictable and the only way in which you can *really* let the team down is by not trying your best – so the way to counter any pressure is to be determined to give it your best shot.

While you are riding the test, you will be super-sensitive to any problems or errors – they will probably feel a lot worse than they look. If you make a mistake, do not dwell on it; once it is done, it is done. Dismiss it from your mind and concentrate on what is to come. The effects of many mistakes can be minimised by clear thinking. If, for example, you misjudge where to prepare for a downward transition, remember that a good transition performed a little late will get a better mark than an 'emergency stop' on the marker. Also, the former will leave you with an attentive, forward-thinking horse whereas the latter will destroy his activity and probably ruin the next movement. If you have a major problem which results in the horse coming completely off the aids, do not panic, get into a fight with the horse or give up mentally: these actions will simply spoil the rest of the test. Instead, reorganise yourself and the horse as quickly and calmly as possible. In this way, you can limit the damage to one or two movements, and give yourself the best chance of producing some good work before the end of the test.

Above all, remember that there is no substitute for experience, and experience is often gained through making mistakes!

REACTION TO THE SCORE SHEET

Everyone naturally wants to do well, but to score really well in a dressage test requires a lot of practice, a lot of skill, full coop-eration from a well-trained horse and, possibly, a bit of luck. It is, therefore, quite rare for competitors to score better than they expected; in most cases, people score less well than they had hoped or imagined.

It is a common reaction for inexperienced competitors to take it personally if they get a lower mark than they expected. They feel that, if they have tried hard, this should somehow be reflected in their marks. However, while there may be some reference to their endeavours in the collective marks for the rider, the hard fact is that the judge is not there to give Brownie points for effort but to assess the *horse's performance as seen*.

This last point is emphasised because the judge must mark what is seen. A judge cannot make allowance for the fact that the horse may be able to perform better in different circumstances. Therefore, if you have a big, powerful Warmblood of excellent conformation, who misbehaves and makes lots of mistakes, you must expect a much lower mark than a plain little Cob who is obedient and accurate.

Another point to bear in mind when comparing your marks to your expectations is that training is about trying to do *as well as possible*, and dressage marking reflects this. You cannot expect a high mark just for performing a movement; to get a good mark, you must do it *well*.

Dressage judges, being human, differ in their opinions, interpretation of a test, and severity of marking. You can, however, learn something of value from the marking of most judges. Bear in mind that, while a good judge will certainly give a low mark if it is due, there will also be a reason given, which may well provide a clue as to how to avoid the error in future. Even if you are disappointed with your overall result, the remarks of a good judge are worthy of respect – if you consider them with an open mind you may well learn something useful.

There is one final point about looking at your score sheet, which can teach a lesson for all training. If you have ridden a good test, do not just take a self-congratulatory look at the movements which earned you high marks – instead, concentrate upon the odd movement where you scored lower, try to work out why, and make it your goal to improve on this. Remember, the secret – indeed the whole purpose – of training is to try to do better tomorrow.